Who Should Read This Book

This book can help you if:

- you have or might have a life-changing illness or physical condition
- you are a loved one—spouse, partner, child, parent, grandparent, friend—of someone facing serious illness, infirmity, or disability
- you are a loved one or caregiver for someone who is aging
- you want to visit someone who is not well and want to know what you should do
- you are clergy, a social worker, or a medical professional
- you are grappling with mental illness or addiction in a loved one
- you are wondering where God is when we confront our frailty
- you want to know how Judaism can help you cope

This book is meant to be picked up and put down when you want. If you are facing a challenge to your body or spirit or taking care of another, you most likely do not have the time or concentration to read a whole book. The ideas presented here come in short passages for you to consider. Although there is a flow through the book from beginning to end, the ideas are grouped loosely and do not have to be read in order.

Part 1 of this book addresses you if you are facing failure of your body or spirit.

Part 2 addresses you if you are a caregiver.

Part 3 addresses issues of family and illness.

Part 4 talks about universal questions of God.

You may only want to read parts that are directly relevant to you, or you may want to try to see something from another person's point of view. Or simply flip to anything that speaks to you, read it, and put the rest away for later. Think of these words as the voice of a friend who is nearby when you are in need. Jewish wisdom is there for you to help lighten your burden when you are ready.

Facing Illness, Finding God

How Judaism Can Help You and Caregivers Cope When Body or Spirit Fails

Rabbi Joseph B. Meszler

For People of All Faiths, All Backgrounds
JEWISH LIGHTS Publishing
Woodstock, Vermont

Facing Illness, Finding God:
How Judaism Can Help You and Caregivers Cope When Body or Spirit Fails

2010 Quality Paperback Edition, First Printing
© 2010 by Joseph B. Meszler

Excerpts from *Sichot HaRan,* "Talks with Rabbi Nachman," translated by Rabbi Aryeh Kaplan, in *Rabbi Nachman's Wisdom* by Rabbi Nathan of Nemirov © 1973 by the Breslov Research Institute. Reprinted with permission.

Library of Congress Cataloging-in-Publication Data
Meszler, Joseph B.
Facing illness, finding God : how Judaism can help you and caregivers cope when body or spirit fails / Joseph B. Meszler. — 2010 quality paperback ed.
    p. cm.
Includes bibliographical references.
ISBN-13: 978-1-58023-423-8 (quality pbk.)
ISBN-10: 1-58023-423-2 (quality pbk.)
1. Healing—Religious aspects—Judaism. 2. Diseases—Religious aspects—Judaism. 3. Care of the sick—Religious aspects—Judaism. 4. God (Judaism). 5. Spiritual life—Judaism. 6. Spiritual healing. 7. Sick—Religious life. 8. Caregivers—Religious life. 9. Judaism—Doctrines. I. Title.
BM538.H43M47 2010
296.3'76—dc22

                                                                    2009044625

10 9 8 7 6 5 4 3 2 1

Manufactured in the United States of America

Cover Design: Tim Holtz

Published by Jewish Lights Publishing
A Division of Longhill Partners, Inc.
Sunset Farm Offices, Route 4, P.O. Box 237
Woodstock, VT 05091
Tel: (802) 457-4000   Fax: (802) 457-4004
www.jewishlights.com

Contents

Introduction

I first encountered serious illness when I was a child. I have distinct memories of my grandmother limping along after her stroke. She spent the rest of her life in a large, overstuffed chair, unable to walk on her own. Her speech was also garbled. She was trapped in her house.

My grandfather was equally trapped. He cooked, cleaned, and occasionally left her in the house with a nurse so that he could go do the grocery shopping, but that was his only outing. Together they would watch television with the volume turned up painfully loud. We were all waiting for her to die, but she lived three more years.

When asked how he was managing, my grandfather usually said, "That's just the cards you're dealt." It was an answer spoken out of despair. My grandfather vacillated between being a dedicated atheist ("No God would do this") and an angry protester ("Why would He put her through this?").

There was a morning ritual, and in the evening it was done in reverse. My grandfather would take my nana from the bed to the chair, and then as the sun set, he would take her from the chair back to bed. First, he would make her sit up. She would throw one arm across his shoulders behind his neck, and he would hold her other hand. Together, they would straighten up, standing in an awkward copy of two dancers in a romantic posture. Slowly they would shuffle across the kitchen to their destination.

The cliché "That's just the cards you're dealt" made me come up with the retort "Well, then I want a new deck." For me, this response was more than just adolescent back talk. I refused to believe in a world of despair with no God or an uncaring one. I intuited that there was a different way of looking at this incredibly difficult situation that also acknowledged the other realities present in the home: the love of my grandmother for my grandfather and his love for her, the devotion and faith that they had in each other, and the love that made my grandfather know without question that if the situation were reversed, she would do the same for him.

Since then, many other family members and friends have faced the reality that inevitably our bodies fail or disappoint us, whether it is through illness, disability, or aging. This also goes for diseases of the mind and emotions, such as addiction and depression. As a rabbi, I am confronted every day with such challenges in people in my community, and it is a continuous task to renew my faith and to find meaning in suffering. Words like "cancer," "dementia," and "wheelchair" challenge not only life but also what it means to live.

FINDING PERSPECTIVE IN THE SPIRITUAL PROCESS OF HEALING

When confronted with human frailty and poor health, it is natural to ask, "Why is God doing this to me?" or "What did I do to deserve this?" Such kinds of questions rest upon a particular kind of belief in God, a belief that God chooses to make some people healthy and others sick. I do not believe, as a faithful Jew, that God is so capricious. My God does not cast lightning bolts.

Rather, I believe in a God who created an imperfect and often unfair world but who is also the Power that makes for life and peace. With this kind of definition of God, in times of challenge we can ask, "Where can I find God in this situation? What powers of life and peace can I harness for my healing?"

The title of this book, *Facing Illness, Finding God,* refers to a spiritual process. I do not believe that God is ever definitively "found." But the search, the finding, can raise our vision from the misery in the mundane to the higher horizon of meaning. When all strength is gone, from where do we find the fortitude to continue on? Why is it that love miraculously makes all situations better? How do moments of transcendence come to be when we are in the worst of circumstances? I believe God is the power that gives us courage, love, and meaning when all else fails. With this in mind, the prayers and ancient sources in this book point us toward a theology of healing.

This book is also for anyone who is confronted with physical infirmity or disability in another person. Here a different question confronts us: How can I reach out to others and help not only their bodies but also their souls? The sick person may be a loved one, or for those in the practice of medicine, it may be those you see professionally every day. It may be a member of the family who is chronically ill for whom you have taken on the role of caregiver, or it may be an acquaintance you are visiting in the hospital. Jewish wisdom, and specifically Jewish law, contains guidelines as to how to interact with someone who is sick and can help us with these tasks. Many synagogues, in fact, have committees for visiting the sick or homebound, so that strangers may reach out to other congregants and make the world less lonely.

The Spiritual Compass of Healing

This book is structured around a saying attributed sometimes to Rabbi Nachman of Breslov and sometimes to Rabbi Levi Yitzchak of Berdichev: "Human beings reach in three directions: inward, to the self; outward, to others; and upward, toward God. In reaching truly in one direction, one embraces all three."

Part 1 deals with reaching inward to the soul when the body fails. You might need help looking inside to confront the new and unwelcome reality you face. You can also find hidden resources within that you can use to cope.

Parts 2 and 3 both have to deal with reaching outward. Part 2 takes the point of view of anyone who can be a caregiver for another person, whether you are a medical professional or someone dropping in on another for a friendly visit. Part 3 takes into account that many times caregivers are members of the family, and the crisis of illness brings out a variety of family dynamics and complexities. These issues are unavoidable when facing illness. Reaching out takes into account relationships that are both distant and intimate.

Part 4 acknowledges that we are all searching, groping upward toward God. But what does the word "God" really mean to you? Do you believe in prayer? Why or why not? Can you imagine feeling God's presence in a hospital room or other difficult setting?

At the end of the book there are three appendices. Appendix 1 reprints a translation of instructions by Rabbi Nachman of Breslov on how to talk to God in trying times. I found them a very comforting tool during one of my times of need. Appendix 2 contains an original annotated translation of the "Laws on Visiting the Sick" in the *Shulchan Aruch*, the most authoritative Jewish law code even today. Appendix 3 translates many of these laws into contemporary guidelines. If you are visiting someone in a hospital or nursing home, seeing someone in crisis, or dealing with a chronic situation, these Jewish guidelines might be of help.

Whom You Will Meet and What You Will Learn

Throughout these chapters, personal stories are used amidst classic Jewish sources. These stories are based on true events, but the names and details have been changed to preserve anonymity. The exceptions are the cases of Rabbi Scott Hausman-Weiss (and his son, Abraham), who gave me permission, and Mr. George Wallerstein, whose memory I would like to preserve.

This is not a book about bioethics. I do not approach issues of abortion, stem cell research, euthanasia, or other controversial subjects, although Judaism has a great deal to say about them. The purpose of this book is to approach health and frailty from a spiritual point of view in learning to cope.

Most of all, I wrote this book for me. I think of my loved ones and pray for their wholeness as human beings. Facing illness can be overwhelming, and it is a comfort to know that the sages of Judaism were thinking through many of these issues for centuries before I ever came on the scene. Health and disease have only the meaning that we give to them, and it is my prayer that God finds this search for *shalom* (peace) worthy.

Acknowledgments

I am grateful to all those who shared their stories with me. I present them here out of respect and love, protecting the anonymity of those who have trusted me. It is a true honor. Most of all, this book is dedicated to my wife, Julie, and my children, Samantha and Justin. It is also dedicated to my family, including my mother, Judy, and stepfather, Allan; and my father, Richard, and the memory of my stepmother, Leslie. Similar to others, we have had our share of facing illness as a family, and it has brought us closer together rather than pushed us apart. Finally, this book has its origins in my learning with Rabbi Julie Schwartz at Hebrew Union College in Cincinnati. I am forever indebted to her.

I thank Stuart M. Matlins, publisher; Emily Wichland, vice president of editorial and production; Lauren Hill, assistant editor; Deb Corman, copyeditor; Tim Holtz, cover designer; Kristi Menter, interior designer; and everyone at Jewish Lights Publishing for enabling me to share these meditations on healing, Judaism, and spirituality, and for their tremendous help.

ABOUT THE TRANSLATIONS

Unless otherwise cited, translations of all Hebrew texts—from the Hebrew Bible and Rabbinic sources—are my own. They reflect my own interpretation, and often how I have translated a biblical text reflects how it is used in a Rabbinic commentary.

Raphael

Support for Your Healing

Angels do not play as prominent a role in Judaism as they do in other religions. This may be because the Hebrew word for angel is *malach*, meaning "messenger." An angel in Judaism is any human being who serves—knowingly or not—as a messenger from God. Angels are not otherworldly winged creatures. An angel is a person.

Several years ago, my wife, Julie, went into the hospital for some surgery that turned into a much longer stay than we anticipated. Thankfully she is completely recovered, but it was a scary time. During this period of our lives, Julie more than once referred to her nurses as angels. They were extraordinary people. They worked around the clock and were genuinely concerned with my wife's comfort and recovery. I am still in awe of people so dedicated to helping others that they immerse themselves in the mess of sickness to selflessly help a stranger feel better. To this day, Julie delivers Girl Scout cookies to the nurses at the hospital in an annual pilgrimage of thankfulness.

I think of Julie and her angels when I read one of the bedtime prayers of Judaism. It is a small poem about some famous kinds of angels:

In the name of the Eternal God of Israel:
may Michael be at my right,

Gabriel be at my left,
Uriel before me,
and Raphael behind me,
and above my head the Presence of God.

Bedtime *Sh'ma, Pirkei D'Rabbi Eliezer* 4

Michael is Hebrew for "Who is like God?" It expresses awe and wonder. *Gabriel* means "God's strength." The poem invokes the desire for awe and vigor to be at our fingertips, in the palms of our hands. *Uriel* means "light of God." This angel symbolizes our need for vision, insight, and enlightenment. We want a light before us to show our way. You can probably think of people who served these roles in your life, who helped you experience wonder, strength, and light.

Raphael is second only to God. *Raphael* means "God's healing." This is a force behind you, supporting you. If this is a bedtime prayer, then this is said while lying down. "Behind you," therefore, means underneath you. Certainly many people who are in need of healing lie on a bed of suffering. Yet the bed holds them up, keeping them from the harsh and uncomfortable floor. Raphael invokes this bed of healing, a comforting, sturdy, yet soft support.

Imagine what it is like to crawl into your own bed. There is a feeling of warmth that cannot be found elsewhere. That "just right" feeling of your mattress, sheets, and blankets when you are tired is the feeling of Raphael.

Now imagine people who make you feel that way, who serve as Raphael for you. For Julie, the nurses served as Raphael as they adjusted her bed, helped her feel more comfortable, and enabled her to endure her trial. They were her support as well as mine. Who supports you in your time of need? Finding Raphael, the faces of those who help you in your healing, is part of your journey toward wholeness.

The people who make you feel supported and whole are your healers. They are the ones who channel the presence of the Most High, who creates compassion.

PART ONE

Reaching Inward

Coping When You Are Ill

My New Normal

What is health? Most people think good health means not having to think about their bodies. Our physical functioning should be, we feel, an assumption of daily living. Putting aside questions of diet or exercise, we do not often think about our bodies and resent it when we are forced to. We do not want to have to think about the functions of our bodies that should be involuntary: our breathing, our heartbeats, our mobility. Being healthy means feeling "normal."

One of the most threatening aspects of illness is that it challenges our sense of normalcy, of how it feels to be alive. "This just isn't me," we might say to ourselves as we lie there in bed. If there is perhaps one law of human nature, it is that we do not like it when things change, when our sense of being "normal" is threatened. It is as if our sense of self is in one place while our body is in another. We may sometimes have trouble recognizing the changed body in the mirror.

If illness is when something in our bodies or minds deviates from being "normal," then healing might be considered a return to that feeling of normalcy. But healing can be an emotionally volatile process. It can be a journey full of angst. Who doesn't want to return to being himself as quickly, painlessly, and effortlessly as possible?

Everyone else can seem to get caught up in our unwelcome change. Being dependent on others can feel awful. Suddenly, we have to think of timetables for medications, and we might need someone to help remind us. We have to think of changing sheets, and we cannot do it by ourselves. We might find ourselves watching more television than we ever used to, "hogging" the living room. We can easily feel irritable or depressed. A person might think not only, "What has happened to my life?" but also, "What am I doing to those around me?"

> If you open yourself to Judaism's wisdom, you might find new paths to healing and a new meaning in your unwelcome circumstances.

If you are casting about for a way to cope with sickness, you can be reassured that Judaism has extraordinary tools and insights that might help you. If you are forced to face illness, you may find that the sages of Judaism have already endured similar trials and have something helpful to share with you in their thousands of years of cumulative experience. If you open yourself to Judaism's wisdom, you might find new paths to healing and a new meaning in your unwelcome circumstances.

Stinkin' Thinkin'

There are several popular myths about illness that are harmful to our physical and emotional well-being.

One myth is that disease is a punishment for something that we did wrong or the ploy of a tyrannical god. People shake their heads and mutter, "Everything happens for a reason."

I do not know whether cancer has a reason. It is a cluster of cells that mutates, violates boundaries, and refuses to die. The scary thing is that your disease may not have any reason in the larger scheme of life aside from whatever meaning you give it. If you despair, then your disease is proof that your life is meaningless. Or worse, perhaps you feel you did something wrong and God is punishing you.

Your past moral deeds have nothing to do with whether or not you get sick. Saints get sick and die. Evil people live long lives. Do not think of your disease as punishment. Just because you are facing a trauma does not mean that you must be somehow deserving of suffering. Among friends I call this "stinkin' thinkin'."

Another harmful myth is that if we pray for ourselves or another, God will reverse the laws of nature just for us and send a miracle cure. You might resort to bargaining with God, saying, "I will never do such-and-such ever again" or "I will go to synagogue every week." Such a belief is founded on literalist readings of the Bible where God physically parts the Reed Sea or rescues us whenever we are in trouble as long as we offer proper sacrifices.

Such literalism, however, is a dead end. Even the most cursory reality check shows that this kind of intervention happens rarely, if at all. Not only that, but this reduces the act of prayer to simply wishing. Prayer is far more powerful and nuanced than that.

> You are part of an amazing, fragile world, and you share in both its amazement and its fragility.

But there is another way of thinking about sickness. Sickness is simply a part of God's imperfect world, part of the price we pay for living and breathing. The privilege of being able to enjoy mountaintops and summer rain is that we are subject to the same laws of nature that they are. Our blood flows the way streams flow. Our breath blows the way the wind carries the clouds and leaves interact with the air. Our eyes take in light the way crystals refract illumination. We are all part of an extraordinary process of growth and decay.

You are ultimately an amazing but small animal with a wonderful imagination. You have a limited life span along with every other living creature. You are part of an amazing, fragile world, and you share in both its amazement and its fragility.

"But I Am Not Used to Asking for Help"

When you are seriously ill, one of the first tasks is to acknowledge that you may feel trapped. Perhaps you find yourself confined to a bed, in your home or in a hospital, where people enter your room without your permission. Within this prison exists another prison; your body no longer does what you expect. Your mind rattles around behind the bars of a disobedient physical shell.

Similarly, loved ones can also become prisoners. You may feel guilty because everyone becomes chained to a routine of medical care, keeping you at home or traveling back and forth to a doctor's office, eliminating the daily freedoms that too often are taken for granted. You might think, "What has happened to their lives because of me?" On a deeper level, you may also become a prisoner of anxiety. Worrying may be your central preoccupation. Even if you do manage to watch some television or partake in some other diversion, you may be unable to get your mind away from feelings of concern, guilt, and anxiety about the future.

In the play *Angels in America*, a Jewish character named Louis calls an ambulance for his lover, Prior, who is dying of AIDS. He discovers a bloody mess all over the floor, with Prior apologizing for having lost control of his bowels. In shock, Louis begins to plead with God for help while Prior tells him that maybe he should not touch the mess or him.[1] The moment is painfully familiar to many who struggle with how our lives become changed by disease. Sickness can be, at its worst, a form of entrapment. Sufferer and loved one alike become prisoners.

> A prisoner cannot free himself from prison.
>
> BABYLONIAN TALMUD,
> *BERACHOT* 5B

The Talmud tells of a famous rabbi named Rabbi Yochanan who was also a healer (Babylonian Talmud, *Berachot* 5b). Jewish lore has it that this man was part of a select circle of sages so holy that they could take a sick person by the hand and heal the person. The grasp of his hand healed others.

One day, one of his colleagues fell ill, and Rabbi Yochanan visited him. Rabbi Yochanan asked his friend whether he had found any solace in his suffering. His friend replied that he could see nothing good in his suffering nor in any divine reward—if it existed—that he might receive for enduring such a trial. It was at this point near total despair that Rabbi Yochanan told his friend, "Give me your hand." As the tale goes, grasping him by the hand, Rabbi Yochanan "raised him up."

We might wonder what the writers of the Talmud meant by Rabbi Yochanan "raising" someone. The Talmud offers no further explanation. Does this mean that he magically healed him? Did he simply lift his spirits for a while? Or did he, as his friend was falling into complete despair, find a way to give his friend hope? Sometimes, simply the touch of a friendly hand, not the examining hands of a doctor but the warmth of a hand offered in affection, can change our whole day. Perhaps Rabbi

Yochanan was able not to end his friend's pain but to counter-balance it with a comforting touch.

The story, however, does not end there.

One day, Rabbi Yochanan himself became critically ill. He found himself on a bed of pain, much like his friend had experienced before. Also similarly, another sage of equal holiness named Rabbi Chanina came to visit him. Echoing Rabbi Yochanan's own words, Rabbi Chanina asked Rabbi Yochanan whether there was any solace in his suffering. Rabbi Yochanan replied that there was none, nor could he find any good in any divine reward he might receive. The sage then took Rabbi Yochanan, the healer, by the hand and raised him.

The sages then ask: Why could not Rabbi Yochanan "raise" himself? If Rabbi Yochanan was a great sage and a great healer who could raise people from total despair to healing, why could he not work a miracle on his own behalf? Why could the healer not heal himself?

The story includes a proverb: "A prisoner cannot free himself from prison."

Rabbi Yochanan, for whatever reason, was able to heal others but not himself. It took someone from the outside to reach down and raise him up.

If you find yourself in a prison, you need people from the outside to set you free. It does not matter if your job or your nature is to help others. Sometimes we think that because we are used to helping others, we should not need to help ourselves. This is far from the truth. We all need the intervention of others regardless of how we might see ourselves. Rabbi Yochanan spells out the moral of the story when he concludes, "When I was on the outside, I could be a source of help to others, but now that I am on the inside, don't I need others to help me?" (Song of Songs Rabbah 2:46).

We can become our own worst enemies by refusing help from the outside, thinking that, as a prisoner who is accustomed to helping others, we can simply break out by ourselves. We too often create our own worst obstacles.

More Than Just
Your Body Is Hurt

Joshua was in a car accident. He had skidded on ice on the road and hit a guardrail. He had hit it hard. At first, Joshua seemed fine. At age seventeen, he was more scared than anything, worried about how he would explain how he had gotten into a car accident to his parents and whether they would take his driver's license away from him. As he looked at the crumpled metal that was once the front of the car, he felt embarrassed as the police car pulled up, lights calling everyone's attention to his corner of the intersection. Then Joshua felt severe abdominal pain where the seat belt had been across his midsection. As the police officer waved to him, he fell down and lost consciousness.

The doctors and nurses moved very quickly. They suspected a ruptured bowel and other complications. His parents were by his side in the emergency room as the doctors prepared him for surgery.

When Joshua woke up, he made a startling discovery. There was a small plastic bag attached to his side. The doctors explained that they had to give him a colostomy. Instead of using the toilet, he would now be using this bag. They hoped in a few months' time, after some of his insides had healed a bit, that they would be able to piece his intestine back together.

Joshua and his parents were crazy with anxiety. As Joshua returned to his life, he found his outlook on everything had changed. He did not have much energy. He spoke very softly and slowly. It was more than fatigue. He was depressed. He also wanted to be mad at someone, but he didn't know at whom.

Some days were better than others. Some days he could lose himself in a good book or a movie, and he felt like his old self. Sharing a laugh with a friend or an embrace from his family made these days easier. Almost always, however, in the back of his mind was the haunting question, "Am I going to be like this for the rest of my life? Can I play sports? Meet girls? Am I ever going to sit on a toilet again?"

> One's spirit can sustain a sick body, but who can bear a broken spirit?
>
> PROVERBS 18:14

At the time of this writing, Joshua's future remains uncertain. Follow-up surgical options are questionable. Joshua is certain, however, that no matter the outcome of his physical condition, he will never be the same because of what he and his family have been through. Every person who visited, every person who prayed, every person who sent e-mails and cards helped sustain him. He would have been lost to despair without the help of others.

There is a proverb in the Hebrew Bible that says, "One's spirit can sustain a sick body, but who can bear a broken spirit?" (Proverbs 18:14). Health and illness are not just physical manifestations; they are also spiritual. They take into account the entirety of a person. We know that there are resources for our body's care, but what do we do for our spirit during illness?

Seeking Healing
Body and Soul

Without a doubt, a great deal of the process of healing is physical in nature. When we encounter an illness in our lives or in another, we often learn more about a part of the body than we ever did before. We suddenly are forced to become "experts" on the heart, the spine, how bones work, the composition of blood, or any of an infinite number of physical characteristics about the human body pertinent to our particular illness. To keep current and on top of a vast body of knowledge, physicians today have to specialize in very narrow fields to become proficient at one specific kind of disease or part of the body. The doctor we go to for our ear, nose, and throat is different from the one we go to for our skin, who is different from the one we go to for our heart, and so on.

Not only that, but in treating illness, we have to deal with what seems to be an endless list of new physical realities. The number of pills we need to take, how much and at what times, their side effects, and how much they cost along with whether or not they will be covered under our health insurance plant us firmly in an often uncomfortable material world. Add different kinds of scans and tests or other kinds of treatments, such as radiation and chemotherapy, and it is easy to become lost in a sea of obstacles without an end in sight. We often cannot look beyond the physical tasks we need to accomplish in trying to return to health.

To help us confront this kind of reality, there is an ancient prayer in Judaism that appears in the classic Jewish prayer book. Its author is unknown. This prayer is sometimes offered in synagogue on a regular basis, and sometimes it is offered in moments of crisis at the bedside of a patient. It expresses hopes about healing that we share with people from all places and times. Although various prayer books of different Jewish denominations may have other versions of this text, the following is one translation from the Hebrew:

> Complete healing is as much about completeness as it is about healing.

> May the One who blessed our fathers, Abraham, Isaac, and Jacob, and our mothers, Sarah, Rebecca, Rachel, and Leah, bless and heal _____.
> May the Holy Blessed One be filled with compassion for him/her, balance his/her temperament, heal him/her, strengthen him/her, revive him/her, and quickly send him/her a complete healing [*r'fuah sh'leimah*], healing of soul and healing of body, among all those others who are sick among the people Israel, in this time and soon. And let us say: Amen.

The most important phrase is "complete healing," *r'fuah sh'leimah* in Hebrew. People may use this term when wishing someone well who they know is ill, such as, "I hope you have a *r'fuah sh'leimah.*" Its common use as a Hebrew phrase by itself indicates that it has more than one definition in English. It implies an entire concept of what healing might mean.

R'fuah sh'leimah means that healing is not only about healing the body but also about healing the soul, the immaterial aspect of a person's being. The anonymous author of this prayer believed it so much that the healing of the soul is listed first, before that of the body. "Complete healing" includes both, and one without the other is incomplete.

Judaism has a long tradition of defining healing in terms of the body and the soul. By understanding a person's self to be made of both body and soul or spirit,[2] Jewish sources imply that there is both a material and an immaterial part of a person's being. There are prayers for both body and soul as part of the everyday morning service:

> Blessed are You, the Eternal God, who heals all flesh and makes wonders....
>
> The soul that you have given me is pure. You have created it, formed it, and within me You sustain it....

The Sages of the Talmud believed that the body and soul are integrated and complementary, both for good and for ill. A Talmudic parable relates that we can think of the body and soul as a blind man and a lame man who are in an orchard. They want to pick fruit from a tree. Neither one of them can do it on his own. The lame man then decides to sit on the shoulders of the blind man. In doing so, he is able to stretch out and pick the fruit for both of them. The body and soul are interdependent forces that work together to sustain our being. They are judged to be two parts of a whole, each incomplete without the other (Babylonian Talmud, *Sanhedrin* 91a–b).

Even the Torah describes God first creating the body of human beings out of the material of the earth and then breathing the "spirit of life" into it (Genesis 2:7). Any pursuit of wholeness, therefore, has to take into account both soul and body.

R'fuah sh'leimah also contains a special nuance by using the word *sh'leimah*. *Sh'leimah* means not only "complete" but also "wholeness" and "peace," because it is derived from the word *shalom*. "Healing" here is not only defined as a thorough recovery of physical health but also indicates a state of being. Being healed implies being whole, being at peace, and being complete. Wishing those who are ill a *r'fuah sh'leimah*, therefore, is really wishing them a recovery of the sense of wholeness in their life that illness has taken away.

In other words, through using the phrase *r'fuah sh'leimah*, Judaism teaches that complete healing is just as much about completeness as it is about healing. Healing is more than the alleviation of pain or accomplishing physical tasks. Healing is also about the wholeness of a person, about the person's *shalom*.

You can follow the doctor's orders, become an expert on a disease, and even return to a world of physical functioning, but you still might not be healed. Your spirit may still be damaged and crying out for help. You still may not have found *shalom* in your life.

I Am Never Going to Be the Same

What does it really mean to see healing in terms of *shalom*, in terms of wholeness? Certainly, much more is implied than the absence of symptoms or even the eradication of a disease. Curing a physical malady is not the same as healing the soul and body.

One possible meaning of *r'fuah sh'leimah*, of wholeness in healing, is restoration. When you catch a cold or come down with the flu, you take a few days off from work, your friends bring you chicken soup, and then you return to life as normal. When you are completely healed, you are restored to life as it was before you became ill. Not only that, but those around you who cared for you and visited you are also restored to life as it was before. They no longer have to spend time worrying about you.

We usually do not consider such an illness worthy of our memory, except in how to handle a recurrence of the same kind of thing in the future, such as deciding which medication worked best. The illness comes and goes, and it barely leaves an emotional mark on us. We are restored to life, and we are unchanged. For such minor sicknesses we are blessed to experience healing as restoration. It is the kind of healing we want and even expect.

For any kind of more serious illness, however, to expect restoration is probably unrealistic. When you experience a serious illness, you are changed. Even if we completely recover our physical well-being, the experience of having lost our sense of wholeness becomes a memory that we push away because it makes us fearful ("I never want to go through that again") or uncomfortable about our sense of self ("That isn't really me"). The more serious the illness, the more profoundly we are affected in our emotional well-being.

Linda, who is fifty-something, leads a busy life. She teaches at the local high school, she has a busy social calendar with her husband, and she has just become a grandmother. Then one day, when she goes in for a mammogram, they find a lump in her breast that they want to biopsy. She tries not to think about it and distracts herself by going about her life as normally as possible. Still, in the shower and when she lies in bed trying to go to sleep, a "What if?" full of panic resounds insistently in her mind.

The biopsy comes back with bad news, confirming all of her fears. She is diagnosed with breast cancer. It is only in one breast, but her family history puts her in the "high risk" category. "Am I going to die?" she thinks. "Is that even possible? Me? I just became a grandmother! What's going to happen to me?" She also thinks of her daughter. As a mother, her first instinct brings her daughter's safety to mind. If she dies, how will her death affect her daughter? Linda also knows her daughter is now one generation closer to this dreadful disease and stands a greater chance of inheriting it. What will be the future of her family?

The doctors give her a number of scenarios as to how to go about treatment. After reviewing all of them and becoming an instant expert on different protocols of chemotherapy, radiation, and surgery, she chooses a double mastectomy. She does so matter-of-factly. She figures this out while holding her husband's hand by the pool as they both face the future together.

Both of her breasts are removed, and she wakes up, realizing that this is not a dream. This is real. She has no breasts. She wonders, "Am I still a woman?" She begins a medium-strength dosage of chemotherapy, plus drugs that will limit the side effects.

Her hair falls out. She has to stop working. She wonders whether she will see her grandchild and future grandchildren grow up. Still, she is alive, and the world looks oddly different and even more beautiful. She notices the sun shining and the trees through the window in ways she never did previously.

Months later, her hair grows back, but it is different than the hair she had before. It is thinner and curlier. She also undergoes reconstructive surgery, restoring the shape of her body so that, with her clothes on, no one can tell what she has been through. She finds that she likes going to services more at her synagogue, and she becomes a "regular." Going seems to calm her. She no longer takes each week for granted.

Linda forms a goal in her mind. It is good to have a goal, she thinks. She focuses on living for the first five years after her treatment because some study says that the majority of people who live for five years after such treatment live the full length of their life span. She returns to work, goes to the theater with her husband, and visits her grandchild.

What does a *r'fuah sh'leimah* mean for Linda? Certainly, it cannot be restoration. Life will never go back to the way it was before. Physically, her body is different. Emotionally, she has new fears. She thinks about her mortality more often now, and she fears being incapacitated or not seeing her grandchild grow up. She is fearful of her daughter inheriting the disease. She also surprises herself in having found new strengths and new friends. A support group introduces her to new allies, and people tell stories to her in hallways and elevators of similar trials they or their loved ones have gone through. She also knows that she is a different person now for having gone through this terrifying experience. She looks at her body in the privacy of her bedroom, and she seeks reassurance about her womanhood both from within and from her husband. Without asking for it, she has been changed into a new person. There are rewards in her newfound strength and wisdom, but she would never wish her experience on anybody. She would rather be less wise and less strong and still have her breasts.

> Wholeness means acceptance of a new body, new emotions, and a new sense of self.

In this context, *r'fuah sh'leimah* can only mean acceptance. Restoration is impossible. Life cannot go back to the way it was before, neither physically nor emotionally. But "complete healing" means not only that Linda is out of physical danger but also that she feels whole again, that she has accepted her new body and her new life.

As she brushes her new hair, puts on a dress, and looks into the eyes of her husband, Linda feels beautiful and attractive again. She no longer thinks of herself as a sick person and does not think about her mortality every day. She does not define herself by having or not having breasts. She can remember the days of her treatment without letting them emotionally debilitate her.

Furthermore, her spiritual life has changed. Her relationship to God is different now. She can no longer skip the prayer for healing in the prayer book at Shabbat services as dealing with other people. It is about her now. She can also no longer accept a theology of God who singles out people for cancer and other people for health. In the waiting room for her treatment, Linda saw too many people, including children, who needed chemotherapy. For God to designate some individuals for cancer is too cruel to accept. She finds that she prays on a regular basis. Rather than wishing, however, she now prays for immaterial things, such as strength, courage, and patience. She prays for God to be a Source of Life and Peace and to well up inside of her and others. At a critical moment, she had decided not to give up and feel sorry for herself but to live. She may not have known it, but her actions echoed Rabbinic wisdom: "As long as there is life, there is hope" (Jerusalem Talmud, *Berachot* 9:1).[3]

For this woman, wholeness means acceptance of a new body, new emotions, and a new sense of self. It means the acceptance of a new life, a new "normal." Some people who face life-changing illness also try to accept new physical limitations. A leg does not move the way it used to. It takes longer to cross the street or go to another room. What used to be a reflexive action now takes some time and thought.

There is also a paradox to such healing. Often, when we think of healing, we think of eliminating pain and frustration. For many people, however, healing cannot mean these things. Instead, healing may mean greater patience. Linda, for instance, may tire more easily, and she could drive herself crazy with the expectation that she should move as easily as she used to. When she calms herself, however, she discovers that there are benefits to slowing down. A cup of tea in the morning is no longer gulped down while looking for her car keys. Instead, it is an activity all to itself. There is time to reflect, meditate, and wonder:

> When my spirit fails,
> When my heart is numb,
> I recall days from before,
> I meditate on Your works,
> Over the creations in Your hands I reflect.
> I reach out my hands to You,
> My soul, like dry earth, for You.
>
> *Psalm* 143:4–6

Identifying
Your Exile

When facing serious illness, it is natural to feel a low amount of energy, a loss of appetite, an inability to concentrate, irritability, and restlessness. This is all part of being injured in some way. It is normal to feel sad and lonely when sick. It is even normal to have feelings of hopelessness or to temporarily lose interest in things you care about. If these feelings last beyond the body's recovery or persist for a long period of time, however, you may also be depressed. If you have these feelings or have thoughts of suicide, you must talk to your doctor about depression.

Depression is a clinical disease. It is too often mistaken for just feeling down, especially when sick. It is nevertheless real and has significant effects on your physical and emotional health. Although it may masquerade under the symptoms of a difficult recovery, depression may in fact be the cause of why you feel so bad.

The good news is that clinical depression is highly treatable when diagnosed. Many people who are clinically depressed recover completely when taking medicine. This is not about a failure of nerve or character. Depression is a result of a chemical imbalance in your body that is beyond your control. Talking to your doctor or engaging in some kind of therapy can be very helpful.

The trick is that depression may be treatable, but people have to admit to it first. Our pride or instincts for denial often prevent what could be a much easier path back toward health. Sometimes we need to get out of our own way to get the treatment we need.

In Judaism, we have a useful metaphor for depression. It is the idea that we were once enslaved in Egypt. The Hebrew word for "Egypt" is *Mitzrayim*, literally meaning "the narrow places." It is the place where the Israelites got stuck in narrowness, trapped and squeezed. For Jews, Egypt is not a country. It is a state of mind.

When we sit around the table on Passover, we talk about how we were once slaves in Egypt. If this literally referred to only a certain geographic area at a certain time in history, this would reduce our Passover seder to a mere history lesson. Instead, we take the lesson personally and say that we were all in the Narrow Place and sometimes we get stuck there again. It is our job each year to leave our own personal Egypt, whatever that may be. The Egypt of our emotions is a narrow place that can have physical symptoms and can really hurt.

> You can return to being the person you want to be, a person filled with joy, thankfulness, and love.

Rabbi Nachman of Breslov teaches that "when a person is depressed, his intellect and his mind go into exile." On the other hand, "joy is freedom."[4] Depression is like Egypt because it enslaves. It exiles us from our better selves. To be able to come out of depression gives us the joy of freedom and the feeling of being close to loved ones and God. It is to come out of exile and return home.

If you are feeling as if you are in exile, that no matter which treatment you receive you still feel empty, anxious, or lost, speak to your doctor about depression. You are not alone, for we have all been slaves in Egypt at one time or another. We all get stuck. But liberation is possible. You can return to being the person you want to be, a person filled with joy, thankfulness, and love. You deserve to go home and enter your own personal Promised Land.

I Am Afraid I Might Die

The priest and writer Henri Nouwen wrote about the frustrations many of us feel when trying to talk about sickness. We want to tell our loved ones something real, deep, and important. We do not want to spend our time on trivialities. Too often, though, our conversations lapse into sports scores or dressing tips.

Nouwen relates how a fellow priest had trouble expressing himself in the face of serious illness. The priest was visiting a woman who was dying, and no one wanted to admit it. He left each conversation with her feeling uneasy.

When relating his frustration to another priest, his colleague responded, "Say—I wonder if you are really aware of the fact that *you* are going to die, too, perhaps not within a year but in any case pretty soon." The truth of this statement stopped all conversation and brought the real issue to light. The priest admitted that what he was really scared of by visiting the dying woman was being reminded of his own mortality.[5]

The fact is, we are all going to die, and whenever it happens, it will likely be too soon. Some deaths are tragic and infuriating. Some are simply sad. Philosophers have spilled gallons of ink to talk about the fear of death, but when we are faced with our mortality, we are speechless.

It is hard to talk about dying. It is hard to face the reality that this might be it. Despite our terror, there is power in being able to name our fear: Yes, I am afraid that I might die. I am afraid of not being able to see the people I love or do the things I love to do, of being cut off from the things that matter most to me. I am terrified, and I do not want to go.

Being sick brings these feelings into such sharp focus that it is hard to talk about them. Talking about dying, however, cannot make it worse. It can only admit the truth of what is hovering in the back of your mind all the time. Perhaps, if you know in your heart not only that you are sick but also that this might be the end, it will be helpful to say so out loud. You might even try to admit it out loud in an empty room just to hear the sound of the words "I might die."

Naming it demystifies it. Death is a part of life. Saying so to a loved one might also be a next step. It might give others permission to admit their fears and have more authentic conversations with you.

There is a gift to this kind of terror. Being shocked into the realization that you will die provides clarity as to what you want and what is important to you. You can no longer pretend that you will live forever and can waste time.

I was called into the hospital room of a man who wanted to talk to a rabbi before he died. When I walked in, the family was stunned that I was there. Apparently, their father was not a religious man and had never asked to speak to a rabbi before in his entire life. He had made his request to see me to a nurse without anyone's knowledge. Maybe this was a product of the dementia from which he suffered? His lucidity was known for going in and out. "This is new," one of them said. Nevertheless, they respectfully left the two of us alone.

I pulled up a chair at the man's bedside. He struggled to express himself. I coached him along. After becoming acquainted, I asked him if he was afraid of dying. He shrugged and nodded a little.

Then I asked him, "What do you want?"

He looked me dead in the eye. "Peaches!"

"Peaches?" I said. Okay, maybe he had lost it. Or maybe the man wants a last meal. Was "Peaches" a boat? A dog? An old girlfriend? A favorite sled?

"Is that all?" I said.

He shook his head. "Peace of mind."

After a few moments of silence, I asked him if I could say a prayer for him. There is a Jewish prayer that is said by the dying. Many Jews do not know that we have our own version of "last rites." It is a mini–Yom Kippur, a prayer of personal atonement. Really, however, it is a prayer for peace of mind.

> We may not want to face the unthinkable, but naming our fear can help.

The prayer is written in the first person. Ideally the dying person says it, but often clergy or a loved one reads it on behalf of another. It contains the *Sh'ma*, the Hebrew declaration of God's oneness:

My God and God of all who have gone before me, Author of life and death, I turn to You in trust. Although I pray for life and health, I know that I am mortal. If my life must soon come to an end, let me die, I pray, at peace. If only my hands were clean and my heart pure! I confess that I have committed sins and left much undone, yet I know also the good that I did or tried to do. May my acts of goodness give meaning to my life, and may my errors be forgiven. Protector of the helpless, watch over my loved ones. Into Your hand I commit my spirit; redeem it, O God of mercy and truth....

Sh'ma Yisrael Adonai Eloheinu Adonai echad—Hear, O Israel, the Eternal is our God, the Eternal is one (Deuteronomy 6:4).[6]

We all want peace of mind. We may not want to face the unthinkable, but naming our fear can help.

When I left the hospital room, I told his children that their father really wanted a can of peaches. Just in case.

Bitterness Can Be a Burden

Sometimes we are our own worst enemies. Depressed because of illness or disability, we feel negative about everything, and it colors how we see the world.

Consider how the Israelites felt when they left Egypt. Freedom, finally! Now they should live happily ever after, right? Now they should not have to work so hard.

Immediately after experiencing the euphoria of crossing the Reed Sea, the Israelites found reason to complain. After achieving a high, they came crashing down low:

> They arrived at Marah ["Bitterness"], and they could not drink the waters from Marah because they were bitter.
>
> EXODUS 15:23

In the plain sense of the passage, these lines mean that the Israelites came to a certain spot and did not like how the water tasted. The waters that flowed there had a sour flavor. A closer reading, however, reveals that the water was fine: "They were bitter." Perhaps it was not the water that was bitter, but the people (*Itturei Torah* 3:129).

When we are filled with bitterness, it is in everything that we taste. This goes beyond our opinion of hospital food. Our negativity can make a bad situation worse and is even contagious to others. Constant complaining and seeing the worst in every situation sap our strength.

> Part of the journey through illness is to try to find the positive in a given situation, even when there is very little to find.

Part of the journey through illness is to try to find the positive in a given situation, even when there is very little to find. Bitterness can only weigh you down. Which do you do more: complain or praise? Encourage or criticize? Compliment or disparage? Thank or reject? We cling to existence for a reason: because we love life. Trying to focus on goodness and what we love, even when things are bad, can create a sense of uplift.

The World Is Imperfect

As was mentioned before, when we become ill or when we face illness in a loved one, many of us ask, "Why is God doing this to me?" Pictures come to mind of Job, who the Bible tells us lost and suffered so that we might all learn a lesson. What lesson are we supposed to learn? Frankly, if illness is supposed to teach something, I personally would rather be less knowledgeable and healthier. Ignorance is bliss.

We might be asking "Why?" as if a calamity is out to get a particular person. Because illness can be so devastating, it is tempting to think of disease as evil. After all, disease is harmful to human beings, destroys lives and families, and causes suffering. We do our best to fight it. Technically, however, we cannot call disease evil because it lacks all moral judgment. Bacteria, viruses, and genetic disorders make no conscious choices. Disease might be the growth of bacteria looking for a place to breed or a virus looking for a host. Much like a lion attacking and killing prey in order to survive, a virus attacks a human being to perpetuate itself. It is unconsciously following its nature. From a Jewish point of view, good and evil can only be the product of human decisions.

Similarly, we also acknowledged that many think of disease as punishment. Sometimes we feel singled out by God for suffering, and we ask, "What did I do to deserve this?" It is true that in earlier times, many people understood disease to be a form of God's wrath. People understood plagues to be moral judgments over communities. Jewish communities would fast and pray in order to ward off diseases, hoping to invoke God's mercy. The Torah specifically states that God will send rain to people who are faithful and drought to those who are not:

> It will be that if you truly listen to My commandments that I am commanding you ... I will give you rain for your land in its proper time, early and late.... Be careful not to be seduced into serving other gods ... [then] there will be no rain.
>
> DEUTERONOMY 11:13–17

Blessing and curses abound to "scare the people straight." This kind of theology was useful when the Jewish people were in exile in ancient times. The suffering-is-punishment way of thinking gained traction when the Israelite people were conquered and sent into exile in Babylonia. If God was punishing them, they reasoned, then they could make atonement and go home. Weeping "by the rivers of Babylon" (Psalm 137:1) because of God's wrath contained within it the hope for forgiveness and restoration.

Taken out of this political context, however, this kind of thinking often does more harm than good. When I visit people in the hospital, my heart breaks to meet those who add to their suffering by thinking they must have also sinned. Moreover, in the face of the suffering of children, who could never have possibly committed any sins deserving of being punished with disease, such a theology can be offensive. Contemporary Jewish theologian Judith Plaskow writes that it is "a misguided attempt to vindicate God at the expense of suffering human beings."[7]

If disease is not evil or God's wrath, then what is it? Something so destructive cannot be dismissed easily. Rather than being evil, disease more rightly ought to be understood as a natural disaster. Much like a hurricane that wipes out homes or a drought that kills a community, disease is a brutal part of the natural world.

Jewish thinkers who were also physicians, such as Moses Maimonides,[8] considered illness to be part of the fabric of nature, with all people being equally susceptible and obligated to maintain their health. Maimonides codified healthy living and the avoidance of illness as part of God's design so that people may serve God properly:

> Since preserving the body's health and strength is among the ways of the Eternal—for to attain understanding and knowledge is impossible when sick—one needs to keep away from things that harm the body and habituate oneself to things that make him healthy and strong.
>
> MISHNEH TORAH, LAWS OF ATTRIBUTES 4:1

Jewish tradition believes so strongly in the sanctity of life that saving a life overrides other commandments. For instance, there are many traditional rules for observing Shabbat. Many traditional Jews will not drive or use electricity on Shabbat. If someone is having a heart attack, however, we are commanded to break those rules to save a life (Babylonian Talmud, *Yoma* 85a–b). Similarly, when fasting on Yom Kippur, certain people with health problems and also pregnant women may not afflict themselves so that they come into danger (*Mishnah Yoma* 8). The Rabbis interpret the injunction to follow God's commandments "and live by them" (Leviticus 18:5) to also mean "and not die by them" (Babylonian Talmud, *Sanhedrin* 74a; *Avodah Zarah* 27b). The commandments of Judaism are supposed to promote life and be a means to that end.

Despite this commitment to promoting life, people looked upon medicine with extreme suspicion for centuries. A Rabbinic proverb is that "the best of doctors deserves hell" (Babylonian Talmud, *Kiddushin* 82a). We can understand this comment when we remember the primitive state of medicine all the way through the Middle Ages up until modern times. Doctors probably killed more people than they cured.

As medical sophistication grew, however, this understanding of disease as moral punishment began to be challenged. People gained faith and trust in the practice of medicine, and they understood disease to be morally neutral. Jewish authorities began to affirm the role of medicine in seeking harmony in living with creation so that people could serve God. Interpreters of the Torah understood certain commandments to imply the need for medicine. For instance, in Jewish law, one who commits violence must be sure that the victim is "thoroughly healed" (Exodus 21:18–19). Rabbis derived from this the permission to heal given to the medical community, as well as from other sources, such as "Do not

> God did not say the world was "perfect." The Torah says "very good." But this imperfect world is still a good place to live. The beauties of nature and the potential for good in human beings outweigh the bad.

stand idly by while your neighbor bleeds" (Babylonian Talmud, *Sanhedrin* 85a on Leviticus 19:16).[9] Eventually, Jewish law saw medicine as absolutely obligatory: "The Torah gives permission to a doctor to heal" (*Shulchan Aruch, Yoreh Deah* 336:1). In fact, the work of physicians came to be seen as a positive way of working with nature, similar to that of a farmer tilling soil to produce the end that God intended.[10] It became understood by many that all people got sick, whether they deserved it or not. And God was understood as the Source of Life, as the Creator of all things, both for good and for bad.

In searching for God in our struggle to live in the world as physical beings who are vulnerable to sickness, we might look back to the very beginning of the Torah, in the first chapter of Genesis. Over and over again, God looks at the world and calls it "good," including light (Genesis 1:4); the seas and dry land (1:10); fruit (1:12); the sun, moon, and stars (1:18); birds and fish (1:21); and every animal (1:25). Just before the conclusion of the sixth day, before God rests, the Torah says, "God saw all that God had made and found it very good" (Genesis 1:31).

It is instructive that God did not say the world was "perfect." The Torah says "very good." It means that this imperfect world, which includes things like renal failure, Tay-Sachs disease, and AIDS, is still a good place to live. It means that the beauties of nature and the potential for good in human beings outweigh the bad. Disease is a part of our imperfect world, but life is still "very good" and still worth living.[11]

Our task, then, in fighting disease, is to seek a harmonious way to live with nature. We want to live longer and healthier lives and to enjoy them as much as possible. We also can come to an acceptance that we are not immortal and that even "very good" things, such as our lives and the lives of our loved ones, must eventually come to an end.

Your Body Is a
House for Your Soul

Life is an imperfect, package deal. It comes with good and bad, and we love the world even as we try to accept its difficulties, including disease. But there is another belief that leads us toward a theology of healing, and it is this: God owns your body, and your soul has borrowed it for your lifetime. Your task is to keep it healthy so that you can return it in as best condition as possible to its true Owner.

There exists a fundamental belief in Judaism that God possesses all things in the world, including each person's body, and we are all responsible to God for what we do with our lives, which are God's property. In the book of Psalms, we read, "The world is Mine, and all that fills it" (Psalm 50:12) and "The earth is the Eternal's and everything in it, the world and those who dwell on it" (Psalm 24:1). Life, then, is a gift that God gives us, and it is to be protected and valued. It is much like something given to us as a trust, and each of us is responsible for our health while our bodies are in our care. Rabbi Hillel of the Talmud understood taking care of our health as a sacred obligation, as is told in this parable:

Once when Hillel the Elder concluded his studies with his disciples, they walked along with him. "Teacher, where are you going?"

"To fulfill a sacred obligation," he answered.

"What is this sacred obligation?" they asked.

"To wash in the bathhouse," he replied.

LEVITICUS RABBAH 34:3

Taking care of our health, even our personal hygiene, is part of Judaism's reverence for the sanctity of life. We show respect for ourselves and God by taking care of the body that God gave us.

Rabbinic lore makes an interesting comparison. There is a statement that "the soul fills the body just as God fills the universe" (Leviticus Rabbah 4:8). Just as there is no place devoid of God's presence in the world, so too are our bodies filled with spiritual potential. Similarly, the metaphor of the soul filling our bodies the same way that God fills the world is implicit in the story of the building of the Tabernacle, also called the Tent of Meeting. This house of God that the Israelites built while in the wilderness was supposed to parallel God's creation of the world. In Exodus 39:32, we read that "the work of the Tabernacle was completed" in the same way that "the work of creation was completed" in Genesis 2:2. God laid out a plan to Moses to build a Tabernacle for the Israelites to carry with them while they traveled. With enormous detail, the Torah narrates very specific assembly instructions for this portable sanctuary. The poles, the fabric, and the precious metals are all described, and they were all supposed to have been donated as gifts by people's free will. It is with this tent that the Israelites might have felt the assurance that God was with them and had not abandoned them.

The Torah speaks to the meaning of the Tabernacle when God says, "Make Me a sanctuary, and I will dwell with them"

(Exodus 25:8). Some have understood this sentence in a radical way. Rather than picture a tent with God inside traveling along with the Israelites, the Sages chose to read the words "with them" as "within them," an alternative and legitimate translation of the Hebrew. The people make the sanctuary, but God is actually found "within them," within the people. The people are the ones who bring God with them into the tent.[12]

If we take this metaphor seriously, our body is supposed to be a house for God. Sometimes our house can get weak and sicken. Elsewhere in the Torah we see this metaphor again: "Something that looks to me like a plague is on the house" (Leviticus 14:35) is a proclamation an ancient Israelite would cry. It was the priests, those assigned to holy tasks and maintaining God's sanctuary, who came to heal both the sick person and the "sick" building. Nevertheless, our bodies are considered holy vessels.

> Would we act differently if we viewed our bodies as sanctuaries for God? Would we understand healing as a holy activity, much like the priests of ancient times?

In this way, many of the Sages considered each person as a microcosm of the universe. Our bodies and the universe are parallel and interconnected. We are all a part of everything, one large organism with God as our soul. Maimonides writes:

> Note well that the entire universe is nothing but one individual being…. [Like the human body] in the universe, too, there exists a certain force that is in control. It sets the

main parts into motion and gives them the driving force to
govern the rest.... That force is God, blessed be His name.
It is because [he is a reflection] of this force that man is
called *olam katan*, "miniature world" or microcosm, for he,
too, possesses a certain capacity that regulates all the forces
of his body. And it is for this reason that God is called the
Life of the Universe.

GUIDE OF THE PERPLEXED 1:72[13]

The universe, our bodies, our souls, and God are all interconnected. Each one is a reflection of the other. Our bodies are to
our souls what the universe is to God.

Would we act differently if we viewed our bodies as sanc-
tuaries for God? Would we think of our health differently?
Would we understand healing as a holy activity, much like the
priests of ancient times? Would we be able to stop and stand in
awe of ourselves and what it means to be alive?

You Have Inherent Worth, No Matter What

Appreciating the world and the body is only part of a theology of healing. We must also learn to love our souls, no matter the human appearance.

Of all life on earth, the Rabbis understand human life to have special value, for human beings are created in God's image (Genesis 1:27). On a very basic level, this means that each human life has inherent worth. The sage Rabbi Akiba put it this way:

> He used to say: Human beings are beloved, for they were made in the image of God. With even more love was it made known to humanity that they were made in God's image, as it is said, "For in God's image did God make humanity."
>
> *PIRKEI AVOT* 3:18

The idea of being made in God's image means that each human being is infinitely valuable and no one can take the value of another's life away. Mysteriously, whether it is through consciousness, our moral capacity, or some other aspect of human

character, Judaism holds that human beings have a special connection with God.

This connection pertains to all human beings with all of
our varieties. The Sages believed that it is a manifestation of
God's greatness that the Divine could be represented with an
infinite variety of unique faces. The Sages make this point with
this analogy:

> A single human being was created ... to declare the great-
> ness of the Holy One of Blessing, for as a person uses a sin-
> gle stamp to make a number of identical coins, the Holy
> One of Blessing used the stamp of the first human being,
> but none of them is exactly like the other. Therefore each
> person must say, "For me the world was created."
>
> *MISHNAH SANHEDRIN* 4:5

In other words, human beings' differences are a blessing, and we are
to appreciate the appearances of all kinds of people. Differences in
ethnicity, appearance, and ability are all to be valued and even
celebrated. This includes people with disabilities.

However, it is hard to say, "For me the world was created," when our body disappoints. Nevertheless, the Sages insisted that each person has inherent worth. Sometimes we do not even recognize ourselves because of the trials we face. But even this new person in the mirror we do not want to accept has meaning and value to God.

> Even this new person in the mirror we do not want to accept has meaning and value to God.

Too often, we can feel useless if we are confined because of illness. "I don't want to be a burden" is easy to say. But you are not a burden. You are a creation of God, capable of inspiring others. You have a unique perspective on life that is worth sharing. You are an image of the Divine.

How We Mark
Moving On

There was a custom among the Jews in Eastern Europe for people who had survived life-changing illness to change their name (*Shulchan Aruch, Yoreh Deah* 335:9). There was a belief dating back to the times of the Talmud in the sixth century that if you changed your name, you might fool the Angel of Death who was pursuing you and thereby confuse the wicked messenger's mission.

On a more profound level, however, later Jewish thinkers found a different meaning in this custom. Changing a person's name after surviving a life-changing illness acknowledged on some level that this was a new person. The individual was no longer the person who lived before becoming ill but had become someone different, someone new. Someone who has faced her mortality.

Today, I do not know of anyone who has changed his or her name after facing an illness. The sentiment, however, is still valid. Instead, we have other rituals for moving on. In doing so, we acknowledge that we all have our scars and they are an important part of us.

One ritual is often referred to in Yiddish slang as *benching gomel*. The word *benching* actually derives from a Latin root, the same as the English "benediction." It is to say a blessing at the end of something. *Gomel* comes from the Hebrew that means "to be kind or charitable." Technically, the two words together refer to a blessing that we say for God's kindness for having helped us escape a life-threatening situation.

The procedure in synagogue goes like this: A person who has come through a life-threatening situation, whether it be an illness, a car accident, or even childbirth, is called up to the Torah. The person says:

> *Baruch atah Adonai, Eloheinu Melech haolam, sheg'malani kol tov.*
> Praised are You, the Eternal our God, Ruler of the universe, who has given me goodness.

The congregation then responds:

> *Amen. Mi sheg'mal'cha kol tov hu yigmal'cha kol tov, selah.*
> Amen. May the One who has given you goodness continue to give you goodness forever.

Most of the time that I have seen and heard this prayer said, I have shared in tears. It is not because the blessing contains moving poetry. It is a simple blessing. It is because to stand on your own two feet, to recognize what a precious gift each day is, and to acknowledge this realization publicly is very powerful.

If something traumatic happens to us, it might be tempting to just try to move on and forget it. It is healthier, however, to acknowledge that on some level you have become a survivor. Judaism asks that we do so publicly. The individual stands with the community, and the community embraces that person. In doing so, we share each other's burdens, lessen each other's sorrows, and publicly show gratitude for goodness whenever we can.

Still another ceremony involves going to the ritual bath, or *mikveh*. This bath is most commonly used for spiritual cleansing to prepare for Shabbat or for women after menstruation. It is becoming increasingly popular to also use the *mikveh* to mark the end of one time of life and the moving on to another. Recovering from illness of any sort is one such occasion.

> Immersing in a *mikveh* is a potent way to represent starting anew.

Immersing in a *mikveh* involves stripping everything off of your body—including jewelry, makeup, nail polish, and contact lenses—to remove any obstacle between you and the water. Stepping down the steps into the bath is like going backward through the days of creation to the time of fluid chaos. Jewish law instructs the bather to duck the head and lift the feet so that for a moment you are entirely suspended in water, much like a fetus. Coming back out, you return to life and the world. It is a powerful combination of symbols and rituals that can truly be transformative. It is a potent way to represent starting anew.

If you are interested in immersing in a *mikveh* and have never done so before, you can contact a rabbi or call the building where the *mikveh* is located. Most *mikveh* facilities have a guide who can help you with the process.

When Waking Up in
the Morning
Is a Miracle

I spoke with a woman who was diagnosed with cancer and given weeks or maybe months to live. She was very honest and open about her situation with me. I remarked to her, "You really are staring reality right in the face." She answered me, "It is like this for everyone, but people don't know it. You never know what is going to happen. It is just that for me, the cover is off and everything is revealed. Anything can happen to anyone at any time."

Her words reflect Jewish wisdom. We are to treat each morning that we wake up as a miracle. The Talmud says that there are blessings we should say each time we get up. Each action of waking up is an opportunity for a blessing, for consciously acknowledging that each moment is a gift. Most Jewish prayer books include these blessings as part of their morning liturgy:

> When you hear the cock crow, you should say: "Blessed is the One who gives the cock the understanding to distinguish between day and night." When you open your eyes

you should say: "Blessed is the One who opens the eyes of the blind." When you stretch yourself and sit up you should say: "Blessed is the One who frees the captive." When you dress you should say: "Blessed is the One who clothes the naked." When you stand up you should say: "Blessed is the One who straightens those who are bowed down." When you step on to the ground you should say: "Blessed is the One who spreads the earth on the waters." When you begin to walk you should say: "Blessed is the One who makes firm each person's steps." When you tie your shoes you should say: "Blessed is the One who has given me all that I need." When you tie your belt, you should say: "Blessed is the One who girds Israel with strength." When you cover your head you should say: "Blessed is the One who crowns Israel with glory."

BABYLONIAN TALMUD, BERACHOT 60B

Each blessing is tied with a morning action. Nothing is taken for granted, beginning with the first sounds of morning and opening your eyes. As you stretch and start the day, you can acknowledge that your body is a miraculous gift. Perhaps it is hard to see your body that way if it is ailing, but nevertheless it is the vehicle through which you experience life. Job said, "In my body, I see God" (Job 19:26).

There are a lot of old jokes about waking up in the morning and checking the obituaries just to make sure that you are not mentioned. Behind this humor is a feeling of gratitude, that each motion we make as we start our day is precious. Imagine trying to maintain that consciousness throughout the entire day, step by step, moment by moment. Saying morning blessings, whether they are the traditional ones in the Talmud or ones of your own writing, can make you more mindful of your days. It can also add urgency to your appreciation of life.

Physical failing can be a catalyst to deeper living. If you have been holding back apologizing to someone or telling a loved one how you feel, now is the time. "Repent one day before your death. How will you know when that will be? Repent then each day of your life" (Maimonides on *Pirkei Avot* 2:10).

If you have been putting off learning that thing that you have always wanted to do, now is the time. "Make your learning a fixed time, say little and do more, and greet everyone with a cheerful face" (*Pirkei Avot* 1:15).

> As you stretch and start the day, you can acknowledge that your body is a miraculous gift. Imagine trying to maintain that consciousness throughout the entire day, step by step, moment by moment.

If you have not said thank you to the people in your life who sustain you, now is the time. "Give to God what is God's, for you and all that you have are God's" (*Pirkei Avot* 3:7).

When Raphael
Makes You Face
Forward

Curing is something that may or may not happen, an issue to be discussed between you and your doctors. Wishing is something you do in despair when you feel alone and want life to be different. Healing is a different matter. Healing happens through your spirituality.

In midrash, or Rabbinic lore, the biblical story of Lot and his daughters is retold. In the story, Abraham's nephew, Lot, lives in a city that is about to be destroyed. Fire is going to rain down from heaven. Two "men," angels, come to rescue Lot and his family. Lot is reluctant to go. The Torah says that one of the men reached out and took him by the hand. Lot and his daughters escape, but Lot's wife cannot face the future, and looking backward, "she became a pillar of salt" (Genesis 19:26), most likely from her tears.

The midrash explains that the "man" who took Lot by the hand was Raphael, who represents the power of healing. It was this touch that gave Lot and his daughters the power to look forward beyond their tears and leave the life they used to know (Genesis Rabbah 50:11).

Real people of flesh and blood can be angels when they are agents of healing. Think of those in your life who have helped heal you in your times of trial. We have all had moments of despair. We have all had nights when the hours seem to creep by without end. Perhaps you have thought that it would be better if it would all just end, that it would be a relief it if were over, even if that meant surrender or suicide.

But then someone touches you. You remember your reasons for living. You remember children or grandchildren. You remember the warmth of the sun on a beautiful day, the thrill of doing something you love, and the comfort of being around the dinner table with family and friends. You face forward and find reasons to live.

From where does your strength come? When you have nothing left, from where do you get the power to keep going?

> Think of those in your life who have helped heal you in your times of trial.

The Rabbinic story of Raphael and Lot is based on a specific phrase in the story. *Vayitmahmah*—Lot "lingered." He was stewing in his disbelief, reluctance, frustration, and despair. God took him and his family, each by the hand, *b'chemlat Adonai alav*—"in God's compassion for him" (Genesis 19:16).

I believe that God gives us the strength we need within ourselves and through those we love when we could just as easily face backward and become a pile of salty tears.

PART TWO

Reaching Outward

Finding Strength in Caregiving

What You Do
Matters

If you go to visit someone in the hospital, whether it be a friend or a loved one, or go to the home of someone who is facing illness, it is common to feel self-conscious and have this inner dialogue: What should I say? Where should I sit? Maybe I should just stay standing with my coat on because I feel uncomfortable....

Physicians are often rated not only on their medical expertise but also on their bedside manner. Doctors go to medical school to study how to cure illness, and they must make time during their careers to try to keep abreast of the latest discoveries and treatments. Rarely, however, do doctors study how to be with someone in a room, where to sit, or how to say what needs to be said.

I have found from working as a congregational rabbi and as a hospital chaplain that many doctors feel completely lost when it comes to delivering difficult or complicated news to patients. Without a member of the clergy or a social worker present, many patients become lost in the language of what is being said, and many doctors feel intimidated by the news they have to deliver. Sometimes people protect themselves by using highly sophisticated jargon to distance themselves emotionally in such conversations. There is a certain amount of wisdom in this for caregivers in that doctors need to be objective and not let their own emotions complicate the situation, but that is not the whole story. When we come to see doctors (and even doctors need doctors), we feel that we are putting our lives into their hands. We are in great need of empathy.

Despite our reservations, visiting someone who is sick is something that we can all do. Judaism considers it a *mitzvah*, a sacred duty. Some synagogues have *bikur cholim* (visiting the sick) or "caring" committees that send people to visit congregants who are ill. We all know people who are in need.

Judaism teaches us specific ways of being in a room with someone who is ill. We can risk entering into a relationship, even if it is only a very brief one, by not only discussing the prognosis but also listening to another's anxieties and hopes. We can become better friends, congregants, doctors, and family members by simply being there when it matters.

Even when facing physical challenges, true healing can only come with healthy relationships. Healthy relationships are just as important as painkillers and other physical treatments. Without these spiritual lifelines, we are left with a deeper level of suffering that deprives life of meaning.

There is a story in the Babylonian Talmud about a famous sage named Rabbi Akiba (Babylonian Talmud, *Nedarim* 39b–40a). He was a teacher known not only for his wisdom but also for his concern for the vulnerable members of society. One day, one of his disciples fell ill. When Rabbi Akiba asked after him, he discovered that none of the other sages or students had gone to visit this man. Even though others might have considered it beneath their station in the academy, Rabbi Akiba went himself to visit his student. He found a very depressed young man.

The student lay there, too overwhelmed with suffering to speak.

Rabbi Akiba began to perform some basic chores for the sick student, including sweeping and washing the floor. As he finished, the student stirred. The boy's weak voice came from the pillows and asked, "Teacher, have you brought me back to life?"

Simple human contact can be life-giving. Menial chores on behalf of people who are ill can make them feel less alone. Sweeping the floor can mean that someone cares, that someone is there to help in some small way. Today it might mean stocking the refrigerator, sorting the mail, or emptying the dishwasher.

> We can become better friends, congregants, doctors, and family members by simply being there when it matters.

More important than doing something is simply being there.

It is for this reason that Rabbi Akiba taught a lesson from his experience that "one who does not visit the sick is like one who sheds blood." This message was later also taught by Rabbi Akiba's student, Rabbi Dimi: "One who visits a sick person causes him to live, and one who does not visit the sick causes him to die." Although this is certainly hyperbole, the intent is clear: showing up matters. Metaphorically speaking, we can revive someone else just with our presence. We have the power to either increase or alleviate suffering by being absent or present. Our relationships are more powerful than we think.

It's Not about You

One of the characteristics that permeates the Jewish tradition regarding caring for those who are ill is sensitivity to the unique circumstances of each person's suffering. This sensitivity is manifest in everything a caretaker does, and rules for how to visit were codified into Jewish law. The most authoritative code of Jewish law is the *Shulchan Aruch*, which was composed by Rabbi Joseph Karo and added to by Rabbi Moses Isserles in the sixteenth century from the myriad rules and teachings in earlier Jewish writings (see appendix 2). For instance, how often you may visit depends entirely on the sick person. If the person asks you as a visitor not to come or to leave, then this should be immediately respected and obeyed. People with certain illnesses that might be embarrassing should also be treated with sensitivity. The Rabbis specifically made mention of intestinal illnesses, impairments to eyesight, and headaches. Visiting people with these conditions might hurt their dignity or might simply make them strain themselves in an effort to be polite when they should be resting (*Shulchan Aruch, Yoreh Deah* 335:2, 8, 10).

Sometimes we want to visit because it will make us feel better. If speech is hard for someone, however, or if it is a hardship to have to interact at a certain moment, then we should not put a sick person in a position of having to talk to us to satisfy our needs. Many times sick people wind up taking care of others when they are the ones who require care. Visiting the sick is not about "us," but rather about "them."

The Rabbis were also very concerned about modesty. Today, hospital gowns allow access for nurses and doctors to be able to reach our bodies unimpaired, but they do not take into account our dignity and sense of modesty. All the more so, a visitor should be sensitive to the compromising position, especially between genders, in which we often find ourselves while in a hospital setting.

The Rabbis therefore offer this very practical advice: when visiting someone who is ill, you should knock first, and if it is not okay to enter, you can either talk to the person from behind the door briefly or simply go away and visit later if the person wants it. The safest approach is to ask whether it is okay to visit, come back later, or not come at all. The *Shulchan Aruch* makes these rules explicit. (Although the Hebrew language assumes a masculine gender, these guidelines apply equally to men and women.)

> Anyone whose sickness is overwhelming and speech is hard for him should not be visited in person, but rather people should come into an outer chamber of the house and ask and inquire of him whether they need to help clean or rinse anything, or similar things, and they should listen to his pain and pray for compassion on his behalf.
>
> SHULCHAN ARUCH, YOREH DEAH 335:8

The Rabbis here caution that we should be sensitive to how overwhelmed a person feels. The phrase here for being overwhelmed literally means that "the world is heavy on him." It is as if the person is "carrying the weight of the world on his shoulders," as a popular saying goes. We should remember that a sick person feels burdened. If we want to be helpful, we can volunteer for chores that need to be completed, and we should try to remember when we should enter into a room with a sick person and when we should respectfully keep our distance. All the more so should this be heeded with regard to touching. Any kind of touch, even as simple as holding someone's hand, should be preceded by a question asking whether it is okay. This also applies to wheelchairs or bed railings, because some may see these as extensions of their body and personal space.

> The Rabbis use a beautiful phrase: we are to "listen to another's pain" (*Shulchan Aruch, Yoreh Deah* 335:8).

We should also remember that even if we do everything "right" and still a sick person sternly tells us to get out of the room and leave her alone, a person in a hospital setting may be looking for a way to vent frustration. Sometimes, a visitor can become the object of a sick person's anger for no apparent reason. Even this, however, can be a service to the ill person. The one person whom a patient in a hospital can control is the person who comes to visit, and if kicking the visitor out of the room lets the patient express her frustration and gives her a feeling of control, then even that visit has done some good. Showing up even to be told not to visit still shows the person that you cared enough to be there.

There are limits as to who may visit, however. The Sages make very clear that sensitivity is also needed in a situation where there is a conflict in a relationship. Although such a vulnerable moment may be an opportunity to reevaluate priorities and make peace with another, more often than not such a person should not surprise another at the door. The Sages caution that you should not visit someone who hates you or with whom you are still in the midst of serious contention. Such a visit might only bring a greater burden and cause more grief. Simply sending a gift might be a more appropriate first step to heal an old wound (*Shulchan Aruch, Yoreh Deah* 335:2).

Finally, in these guidelines for visiting the sick, the Rabbis use a beautiful phrase: we are to "listen to another's pain." Perhaps the greatest contribution we can make to other people's welfare, aside from making sure that they receive good medical care, is to listen to their suffering.

"Don't Just Do Something. Sit There!"

There is not much to do when we visit someone who is sick. In fact, when we visit someone who is ill we are asked to do something that may not feel natural to us or, even worse, something we may find boring. We are asked to sit and listen.

There is a remarkable skill that has been developed in modern culture, a skill that today's child learns, some even before learning to talk. It is not "multitasking" or even "downloading." This extraordinary talent is the ability to "tune out."

Tuning out is the ability to pretend that you are listening to someone talking while your mind is elsewhere. In a world where everything has become faster and the amount of information with which we are inundated multiplies exponentially, all of us eventually learn to listen selectively, snapping to attention when we hear our name and know that the conversation suddenly relates to us.

Most of us have had the experience of being on the phone, pretending to listen, while the person at the other end of the line seems to drone on and on, until suddenly we realize that the person is pausing, waiting for our response, our "uh-huh" or grunt of affirmation, and we realize that we have been caught tuning out. We all also know what it is like not to be listened to, to hear another's answer come to us a few beats later, to realize that the person was watching television or even typing on the keyboard instead of listening to what we had to say. Imagine how this feels when we are ill and seeking some kind of connection with another. This kind of half listening is inadequate when visiting the sick.

Although tuning out is a skill of survival in a world of chatter, television commercials, and constant background noise, the price for this line of defense is that many of us forget how to listen. It is easy to forget that listening is an actual activity, and not a passive one. Real listening does not only mean taking in all of the information that is being said to us. It also means reading the facial expressions of the speaker and being sensitive to her tone of voice. Most importantly, active listening means making the other person feel heard. The importance of listening only increases when we know that the person with whom we are visiting is suffering.

> If we learn to listen deeply enough, we might hear through the voice of another an inner sound so deep that we remember who we are and from where we come.

After all, let's face it: often we do not listen because we do not want to, because the conversation is not about us. So many people are constantly fighting for our attention, and we want to focus on ourselves and what we want. Sure, we perk up when our name is said, but to pay attention to someone else's cares and concerns that have nothing to do with us is a real effort.

Even knowing that another is in pain does not necessarily break through the wall of self-absorption that surrounds many of us. "What does this have to do with me? How long is this going to take?" These are questions we ask ourselves not just when we go to visit someone who is ill. We often ask ourselves these questions when it comes to paying attention to our children, parents, or other loved ones. The act of listening is an important way of connecting with others spiritually, and yet we are often too wrapped up in ourselves to notice. Perhaps it is for this reason that Rabbi Nachman of Breslov once taught that if we are sitting in a chair but our minds are elsewhere, not listening, then our chairs are essentially empty (*Likutei Moharan* 1:21).[1] We are spiritually absent.

Listening is a spiritual activity. It is about the other, not about us. Meditation teacher Sylvia Boorstein puts it this way: "Don't just do something. Sit there!"[2] All true religiosity begins with being humble enough to listen. It begins with realizing our smallness in relation to others, to the universe, and to God.

Humility is the opposite of self-absorption. It is the antithesis to the arrogance that we do not have to listen because we already know what another person has to say. Humility in action is listening, truly listening with the soul. It is to make ourselves vulnerable to what another person has to say and to be sensitive to what is struggling to be said. What words have found their way to the surface, and what words have not? Humility is the start, the doorway to other spiritual opportunities. In terms of visiting the sick, humble listening is essential. The Rabbis do not say, "Listen and take down notes of all the information the sick person is relating." We could do that with a tape recorder. Instead, we are to make human contact and make the other person feel listened to. This is what the Rabbis meant when they said, "Listen to another's pain." Hearing pain implies a relationship.

The commandment to listen does not just appear in the laws for visiting the sick. It also appears in the most important place we can find in Judaism, and yet we can take it for granted and do not think about it: *Sh'ma Yisrael Adonai Elohein Adonai echad*, "Hear, O Israel, the Eternal is our God, the Eternal is one" (Deuteronomy 6:4). The central statement of monotheism, the belief in one God, begins with this phrase: "Hear, O Israel." The statement does not say, "See" or "Look." It does not tell us to "realize" or "understand." It says, *Sh'ma*, "Listen." We should listen so that it changes us and who we are. We should be open to the other, and to all the others that lead us to the Eternal One. The gateway to God in the *Sh'ma* begins with listening. Hearing is the first spiritual step.

And, perhaps, we might take comfort in the belief that God also listens to us. Children often ask in religious school why it is that God does not seem to talk anymore the way that God used to in the Bible. In the Torah, God seems to talk all the time, and in quite articulate Hebrew! How come we do not hear God like that anymore?

The answer might be that God is busy listening to us. God is not chattering or tuning out; God is paying attention and listening deeply to us, not interrupting us as we stutter our hopes and fears. God is the Great Listener, the One who hears us no matter how softly we whisper or where we are. God hears all the prayers of our hearts all the time.

And maybe God does occasionally talk and we can hear God's voice, when we are quiet enough. It may or may not sound like articulate Hebrew, but if we learn to listen deeply enough, we might hear through the voice of another an inner sound so deep that we remember who we are and from where we come. If we are humble enough, we may hear God calling to us, begging us not to tune out but to pay attention to the miracles that happen every day in our lives, brought to relief in the face of suffering.

Learning to Listen

Years ago, I was serving as a chaplain in a hospital in Cincinnati. When I was first learning about how to visit people in the hospital, I was very unsure of myself. I would "do my rounds," and, feeling nervous and self-conscious, I would look at my watch and measure exactly how much time I needed to spend and how quickly I could leave. With so much to do in a busy life and so many chores to accomplish, I sometimes wanted to rush in and rush out of these awkward situations.

For some time I was assigned to make visits in the cardiology wing. There were many people there, and not all of them had heart disease. One day, when I was rushing through, I met an old man named George. I don't know what caught my attention about this man, but something made me stop and listen to him. George was at the end of his life, and something in his face told me he knew it. Upon introducing myself, I somehow got lost in a long and wonderful conversation. I forgot to look at my watch. Through some inner compulsion, I was able to lose myself in listening. Even though I was considerably younger than he was, at that moment it did not matter. We were simply two human beings, one talking, the other listening. It was a moment of grace in my life.

George was a war veteran, and he loved to tell stories of his time in the United States Navy. Often, during his stay in the hospital, his mind would wander to his younger days in the service. He told me that he often felt that his current sick body was not the "real" him, but rather he was really still a young soldier at sea. I imagine that sometimes George looked in the mirror and was startled not to see a young soldier but an old man.

What I also discovered, during my one visit with him, was that he was also a poet. He had loved to write poems his whole life and had kept notebooks of his poems in his attic. Unfortunately, somehow during the move from his house to an assisted living facility, all of his notebooks had been accidentally thrown away. He lost a lifetime of his writing. It was not just that he had lost his health and his familiar surroundings; it was also his legacy of poems that he mourned.

> If I had not been fortunate enough to be able to slow down, pay attention, and listen, then George's last poem would have been lost forever.

George, however, had a very good memory. When I asked him if he could recall any of his poems, he immediately began to recite one. I was so impressed that I made him repeat it slowly so that I could write it down. It seemed to capture so much of what it feels like to age and to lose a sense of self in illness. I offer it here:

The Addled Thoughts of an Old Combat Man
I'm sitting alone on the deck of this ship
Just watching the sea and the spray.
There're clouds in the sky, Mom is alive,
And I'm twenty-seven today.

I see the smoke from the beaches
And the tracers that light up the sky
I hear the whine and the noise and the roar
Of the planes going by.

How long have I been here? I don't know.
There are still certain things hard to find,
And the things that I see most clearly
They tell me they are all in my mind.

They say that I'm old. They say that I'm sick.
They're coming to take me away.
They don't really know that Mom is alive,
And I'm twenty-seven today.

In George's mind in the hospital, he was not really an old man, forced from his home, taking medicine for heart disease. Instead, it was his twenty-seventh birthday, and he was in the Navy on a ship, anticipating a letter from his mother.

And if I had not been fortunate enough for some inexplicable reason to be able to slow down, pay attention, and listen, then George's last poem would have been lost forever. I consider myself lucky for having been able to pay attention and listen that day.

And I also believe that God, the Great Listener, heard George's poem, too.

How You Can Be
"On the Level"

In the Rabbis' writings about visiting the sick, they were very specific about how to behave when the ill person was lying down. In earlier times, a sick person would lie down on the floor, presumably on a blanket. There were not rows of beds with curtains between them, as we have now. The Rabbis tell the visitor where to sit:

> When one visits the sick, one does not sit on the bed, on a chair, or on a bench [so that the visitor is above the sick person looking down], but rather one enrobes oneself and sits before him [down on the floor with him], for the Divine Presence is above the sick person's head.
>
> *SHULCHAN ARUCH, YOREH DEAH* 335:3

The idea is that you should not be above a sick person looking down, but on his level. If he is on the ground, then you should be on the ground. In fact, in later years, when beds were man-ufactured more easily, this principle of being on the same level became explicit in Rabbinic literature, as Rabbi Moses Isserles elaborates:

This [rule of sitting on the ground] only applies when the sick person lies on the ground, so that [if one sat in a chair] one would be higher than him, but if he is lying in bed, it is permissible to sit on a chair or bench [and thus they would be on the same level].

SHULCHAN ARUCH, YOREH DEAH 335:3

We are supposed to be on the same level of someone who is ill. We are supposed to be neither above nor below. Rather, we are supposed to be able to look her in the eye.

A principle of the laws on visiting the sick is the equality of all people. A person of great wealth and social standing is supposed to visit another of less wealth or lower social status, and when we visit, we are supposed to physically put ourselves on the same level as the person who is sick. Illness is a great equalizer; no one is immune no matter what family background, prestige, or fame he might enjoy. We all have physical bodies that have limitations, and we all face challenges with health sooner or later. Being on the same level represents equality as physical creatures.

> You should not be above a sick person looking down, but on his level.

The Rabbis imagined God's Presence to somehow be floating above the sick person's head. It would be a mistake to literally think of God as a physical manifestation like a cloud, but nevertheless the Rabbis invite us to think of this figuratively. The implication seems to be that if we are above a sick person looking down, we are presuming to be in God's place. By looking down on those who are ill and forgetting to be humble enough to put ourselves on their level, we are, in a sense, "playing God."

In addition to this social lesson of equality, forcing ourselves to physically be on another's level teaches us about empathy. To get down on the floor with those who have been laid low means to empathize with them. Empathy means sharing in what another is feeling. Without being emotionally available and open, the power of our visit becomes severely limited. To empathize, however, means to help unburden others of their pain and anxiety.

It is easy in an uncomfortable situation to engage in chitchat. We can talk about the weather, sports, or our jobs. These are the topics of a social visit. Given the choice of not visiting versus showing up and talking about trivialities, showing up is certainly the better option, but if we try to listen to how another is feeling, we can aid the person in healing. Naming emotions that we hear, such as frustration, exhaustion, pain, loneliness, or despair, helps alleviate those hurts. Staying with the emotions of a conversation, and being unafraid to be emotional oneself, creates a greater human connection.

How do we keep our conversations on how another is feeling and not on gossip? When people tell us about their illness, we might say, "Wow, that sounds awfully frustrating" or "You sound exhausted and sad" or "You must be lonely." We might even say, "I am sad that you have to face this." We can ask, "How are you coping?" or "Where are you getting the strength to face this?" These attempts to reach out can be enormously helpful to someone whose spirit is burdened.

A Hasidic story relates a time of deep listening to a person's soul. It features the founder of Hasidism, Rabbi Israel ben Eliezer, known as the Baal Shem Tov, or "Master of the Good Name." It was believed that by knowing God's good Name, a person could work wonders.

The Baal Shem Tov was passing through a town in which a man lay critically ill. Word of the Besht's [an acronym for Baal Shem Tov] arrival spread quickly, and the man's doctor asked the Baal Shem Tov to visit his patient.

The Baal Shem Tov came to see the man and looked at him for a brief moment. He then turned to the man's wife and asked her to prepare some chicken broth for her husband. The man sipped some of the soup and immediately began to speak. The Baal Shem Tov stayed with him for a few hours, during which the man's health returned.

As the Baal Shem Tov prepared to leave, the man's doctor asked for a moment of his time. "I know that this man was close to death," the doctor said. "There was nothing I could do, and certainly chicken soup would not be enough to cure him. What did you do?"

The Baal Shem Tov said: "Illness appears in the body but is caused by the spirit. You looked at the man as a body; I looked at him as a soul...."

"And the soup?" the doctor asked.

The Baal Shem Tov simply smiled, shrugged, and took his leave.[3]

As long as we remember that we are listening to souls and not just bodies, we cannot go wrong in our visits with the sick.

You May Not Be Able to See the Difference, But It's There

Do we really make a difference? Many times, when we are facing illness in another, it seems as if we do not. We might ask ourselves, "What difference do I really make?"

A friend is in the hospital. You visit. You walk through the door, give your friend's name at the information desk, and then go to the elevator. Coming out of the elevator, you approach the nurses' station, where they ask you how they can help you without looking up from what they are busy doing. Eventually, you find your friend's room. She is sleeping. She wakes up and greets you, but she thanks you for your visit and explains she is not up to having visitors right now. You realize that now is not a good time. You leave with the hospital smell of antiseptic cleaners clinging to you.

Have you made a difference?

The Sages of the Talmud were passionately convinced that visiting someone who is ill does make a difference, even if the exchange is minimal. Consider the following passage:

It was taught in the Mishnah: "There is no measure for visiting the sick." What is meant by "measure"?

Rabbi Joseph offered, "It means that there is no measuring the enormity of the reward."

Abaye [disagreed and] said to him, "Is there a way to measure the reward for fulfilling any of God's commandments? In fact, have we not learned that we must be as cognizant of an easy commandment as a difficult one, for who knows what the reward will be for each?" (*Pirkei Avot* 2:1).

"Rather," Abaye continued, "['Measure' means that] even a person of great social status goes to visit a person of minor social status." [That is, there is no "measuring" the kind of person one should visit.]

Rabba taught, "It means [that there is no measuring how often one should visit, and] one should visit even one hundred times a day."

Rabbi Acha,[4] the son of Rabbi Chanina, said, "One who visits a sick person takes away one-sixtieth of the sick person's pain."

The sages responded, "If so, let sixty people come, visit, and restore the sick person to health!"

He answered, "One-sixtieth is like the fraction spoken of in the school of Rabbi [where each person takes away one-sixtieth of the remainder, not the original]. Further, the visitor must be of the sick person's same affinity."[5]

BABYLONIAN TALMUD, *NEDARIM* 39B

In order to understand the many things that are going on in this passage, you have to read it step-by-step. Different rabbis have come together to try to understand what a certain proverb means. In the very first collection of Rabbinic law called the Mishnah, completed by 200 CE, there is a saying that "there is no measure for visiting the sick." The rabbis are asking what "measuring" means here. What is this sentence trying to teach us?

The first sage to offer an answer is Rabbi Joseph. He states that "measure" refers to the reward. There is no measuring the enormity of the goodness God will give us if we visit the sick. If we visit someone who is ill, who knows what will come of it? We might have participated in another's healing, we might have given the person comfort, or we might walk away changed ourselves. There are unlimited rewards for fulfilling this commandment.

> Rabbi Acha said, "One who visits a sick person takes away one-sixtieth of the sick person's pain."
>
> BABYLONIAN TALMUD, *NEDARIM* 39B

Another sage, Abaye, disagrees. All of this is true, Abaye argues, but the same could be said for fulfilling any commandment. Giving charity, offering hospitality, or any virtuous act can result in immeasurable positive consequences. This proverb, however, refers specifically to visiting the sick. He therefore concludes that it has to do with a kind of measuring that people do to each other. Sometimes people "size up" each other to see whether something is worth their while. Is visiting someone worth my time? Abaye says that the answer is always yes. Regardless of status, we are all equal in the eyes of God and also all equally susceptible to illness. Being able to get sick is common to all humanity, regardless of gender, wealth, or age. Therefore, visiting the sick should be incumbent upon all people equally.

Another sage, Rabba, has a different idea. He thinks "measuring" has to do with counting how often you should visit. By

saying there is no "measure," he says that given the right circumstances, a person could visit even a hundred times a day.
Later Jewish law would clarify that this holds true as long as it
is not a bother to the sick person (*Shulchan Aruch, Yoreh Deah*
335:2).

The final explanation, offered in the name of Rabbi Acha,
whose father was also a rabbi and perhaps taught him this lesson, presents a completely different interpretation on "measuring." Rabbi Acha believes "measuring" refers to the effect we
might have on someone who is ill. He states that when you
visit a sick person, you take away one-sixtieth of the person's
pain. To understand what he meant by this, we must understand what the Rabbis meant by "one-sixtieth."

Rabbi Acha and the rabbis of his time used the fraction
"one-sixtieth" as a metaphor. For the Sages in ancient times,
one-sixtieth was the smallest possible measure of something to
constitute something real. If something was less than one-
sixtieth, it was as if it did not exist. Once a measure of something
reached the proportion of one-sixtieth, it had significance. For
instance, in Jewish dietary laws it is forbidden to mix milk and
meat. If you are making a meat stew and somehow a drop of
milk accidentally falls into the pot, if the proportion of milk to
meat is less than one-sixtieth, it is as if the drop does not exist
and you can eat the meat stew without any problem. If it is
one-sixtieth or more, however, the stew is no longer kosher. In
many contexts, the Rabbis refer to one-sixtieth as the smallest
fraction, the smallest hint of something. They believed, for
example, that the experience of a dream was like one-sixtieth
the experience of prophecy and that sleep was like one-sixtieth
of death (Babylonian Talmud, *Berachot* 57b). Of course, a
dream is not the same thing as a prophetic vision, and sleep is
not the same thing as death, but we get a hint at what those

larger experiences are like by living through the smallest possible fraction of them.

When Rabbi Acha states that a visitor takes away one-sixtieth of another's pain, therefore, he is saying that the visitor makes an indiscernible but real difference in the sick person's life. Simply by showing up, the smallest bit of reality is changed for the person facing illness.

Some sages respond to Rabbi Acha's teaching that if this is true, then why have medicine? Let sixty people show up, cure the person who is sick, and be done with it! Unfortunately, Rabbi Acha explains, life does not work that way. Each successive person who appears takes away one-sixtieth of the remainder of someone's pain, not the original whole. Medicine is needed to cure a person, but each person who visits takes away a small fraction as well.

Not only that, but there also has to be some kind of connection made between the sick person and the visitor, that they be of the same "affinity." If the visitor is a complete stranger with nothing in common and does not reach out to make a real connection, such as an orderly who comes into the room to absentmindedly take the patient's blood pressure, then the sick person is not helped. If someone comes to actually visit and inquire about a sick person's welfare, however, the visitor takes away a small but real amount of the other's suffering.

Do we make a difference? It may not appear so, Rabbi Acha teaches, and it may not be measurable in a medical sense. The emotional and spiritual reality, however, registers a change in the sick person's life. Each one of us makes a difference, even though we may not be able to see it.

Even God Visits the Sick

The term for "visiting the sick" in Hebrew is *bikur cholim*. By considering such an act to be a *mitzvah*, the Rabbis were saying that visiting the sick was more than just a good deed that you perform in your surplus time. Instead, being with the ill is something God wants and commands us to do. To emphasize the importance of this commandment, they explained it in these terms:

> Rabbi Chama said in the name of Rabbi Chanina: What does the following verse mean: "You shall follow after the Eternal One your God" (Deuteronomy 13:5)? Is it actually possible for a mortal to follow after God's Presence in this world? Does it not also say: "The Eternal One your God is an intense fire" (Deuteronomy 4:24)?
>
> Rather it means to follow after the Holy Blessed One's attributes…. Just as the Holy Blessed One visits the sick, for so it says, "The Eternal One appeared to him [Abraham] by the oaks of Mamre" (Genesis 18:1), so should you visit the sick.
>
> BABYLONIAN TALMUD, *SOTAH* 14A

This complicated passage contains a very important message about what it means to visit the sick. One rabbi, Rabbi Chama, teaches a lesson that his teacher, Rabbi Chanina, taught him. He begins by quoting a verse from the book of Deuteronomy and asking what it means: "You shall follow after the Eternal One your God" (Deuteronomy 13:5). The literal meaning is unacceptable to him. People cannot follow God the same way that you follow a person on the street. God is not a person in whose footsteps we can follow. Not only that, but it also says in the very same book of the Torah that God is a power similar to an intense fire, and to play God is like trying to follow a rocket. You will get burned.

> We do not have to know the right thing to say or feel that we have to be specially trained in order to be with those who are ill.

Rabbi Chama explains that rather than meaning literally walking in God's footsteps, the Torah means "following after" the way that children follow after their parents or the way students follow after their teachers. It means imitating. The Rabbis believed that God demonstrated certain actions for us to follow or imitate, called "attributes." One of these attributes was visiting the sick.

According to Rabbinic interpretation, after Abraham circumcised himself at age ninety-nine (without anesthesia or sterilized surgical tools!), God appeared to him in a forest of oak trees in an area called Mamre. It does not say in the Torah that God did anything but appear. It simply says that God showed up. (This is highly unusual for a biblical narrative; if God appears, it is usually to say something.) The Rabbis read into these verses that Abraham was convalescing from his surgery, and God appeared to him to comfort him. The Rabbis believed God did this to demonstrate the importance of visiting the sick. Rather than just give us a commandment in a "thou shalt" form, God wants us to do this so much that it is as if God said, "Do not just do what I say; also do what I do."

What the Rabbis teach is that visiting the sick is of extraordinary significance. They felt that those who tend to the ill are imitating God in some way. To be with and participate in another's healing is "God-like" without going so far as to "play God." To be more than "God-like" is impossible; it even invites getting burned. Perhaps trying to work miracles for a sick person might risk this kind of "burning" in the form of some kind of physical or moral disappointment.

Perhaps the best guideline is to be found in the idea that God showed up but did not say anything. This means that we do not have to know the right thing to say or feel that we have to be specially trained in order to be with those who are ill. Being with someone is enough.

Emotional Disorders and Addictions Are Jewish Problems, Too

People used to whisper the words "cancer" and "stroke" as if speaking them aloud were tempting fate. People now talk more openly about these kinds of illnesses. However, when it comes to an emotional condition such as bipolar disorder or alcoholism, we still drop down to a whisper. Our community and families are tested when dealing with severe emotional problems because there is still a strong social taboo against talking about them.

These conditions are diseases like any other, only they are distinguished by how little we talk about them publicly. This is especially true in the Jewish community, where it seems forbidden to admit that we have an emotional or substance abuse problem. Three examples highlight the need for us to take bold steps to acknowledge that these are all part of the Jewish community and need to be addressed.

A doctor needed to spend a few nights in a hospital for depression. His wife did everything she could to keep what had happened secret for fear that if word got out he would lose his practice. She was absolutely petrified that people would flee from being his patients if they knew he had spent those nights in the hospital for a "mental illness." My guess is that she had good reason. It turned out the man simply needed to have his medicine altered, but nevertheless the family decided not to talk about it with anyone. Fortunately, they confided to me about what was happening, and I was able to visit the man while he was in the hospital. Later, the family said the visit was a tremendous lift to his spirits and helped with his healing. I am sure it had less to do with me personally than it did with the relief they felt in finally revealing their secret to someone who would understand.

> Through forming bonds and relationships, those facing addiction can find the strength to combat their disease.

A second example comes from every school, synagogue, camp, and other institution dealing with youth. More and more children are now diagnosed with different kinds of disorders and emotional challenges, and many of them take medication. There is a great benefit to catching an emotional development early in helping a child learn to live with it and overcome it. But to be labeled a child with "special needs" creates an opportunity for teasing and bullying. If we as a community do not talk openly about tolerance and inclusion of those who seem to be different, then we are adding more of a burden onto a child who already is carrying a great deal in life.

For a final example, a mother and father came to me to talk about their teenage son. The couple looked exhausted just walking through the door. They came with the news that their son had been diagnosed with bipolar disorder or what used to be called manic depression. This had taken years of bringing him to various treatment centers. When he turned eighteen, he moved out of the house. Not being able to control his impulses and having the immaturity of an adolescent, he had turned to smoking pot, drinking, and then using harder drugs to bring him down when he felt high and to lift himself up when he felt low. These "solutions" had become problems in and of themselves. After years of being unable to find a remedy, the parents had to resort to changing the locks on their house so that their own son could not break in and steal from them in order to feed his habit.

This mother and father truly were suffering. Both they and their son needed prayers just as much as anyone in a hospital with a heart condition. Both the parents and their son needed support groups of their peers to be able to talk freely about their problems. In fact, emotional illnesses can often only be addressed with spiritual solutions. Alcoholics Anonymous or its Jewish equivalent, JACS (Jewish Alcoholics, Chemically Dependent Persons, and Significant Others), uses a faith-based program to help people in need. After accepting that your life has become unmanageable, the next steps are belief in a Higher Power and turning over control of your life to that Power's care.[6] It is also vital that you talk openly about your condition with others. Through forming bonds and relationships, those facing addiction can find the strength to combat their disease.

It is easy to think of illness as something that happens only in a doctor's office. This is a mistake. We need to broaden our understanding and reach out to those who suffer emotionally as well, acknowledging that in this regard Jews are no different from any other people.

Be Who You Are and Do What You Know

In one of my chaplain internships, I was required to visit all the Jewish patients in the hospital. The patients were listed by room, and the Jewish ones had a "JW" marked next to them on my register. I made my rounds each week before Shabbat on Friday.

One particular woman caught me by surprise. I looked down at my register and made sure that there was a "JW" next to her name. Yes, there it was. I was confused because the woman was African American, and although there are Ethiopian Jews and Jews who have converted or were adopted, it was still very rare to meet an African American Jew. Shrugging my shoulders, I sat next to the old woman. Although it was rare, it was certainly not unheard of, and there it was on my register. The nurses knew nothing about the patient.

The woman had a tracheotomy, meaning that she had a tube inserted into her throat. She was hooked up to a respirator to help her breathe. As a result, she could not talk. Each week, I visited her. I never bumped into any family, and the notes I left with my phone number drew no response. I would come each Friday and, not being able to enter into any kind of conversation, would sing some songs in Hebrew to prepare for Shabbat. After a few minutes of singing, I would wish her "Shabbat *shalom*," a Sabbath of peace, and leave the room, only to see her next week.

> Even the most tangential of relationships might be important.

At about my fourth or fifth week into my visits, I bumped into a new nurse who was tending to the woman. Again, the nurse could give me no information regarding the woman's background. As the nurse left, however, I overheard her say to another, "Remember, no blood transfusions."

It was then that it all clicked. Apparently, there had been a mistake in the admitting office, and they had confused the "JW" symbol for "Jewish" patients with "Jehovah's Witness." For weeks I had been singing in Hebrew and wishing a "Shabbat *shalom*" to a woman who was a Jehovah's Witness! Because of the tracheotomy, she had been subjected to my off-key singing and Hebrew prayers, helpless to tell me I had made a mistake.

The next week I did not visit. The week after that, one of the nurses caught me in the hallway and told me that this woman was not doing well. She asked me if I would come by because the woman had no other visitors.

I visited, and I was at a loss. What should I do? All of the prayers I knew were in Hebrew. Leaving it in God's hands, I sat down and sang the Shabbat songs again, hoping that she found some comfort in them and that they did not upset her. "One who visits a sick person causes the person to live, and one who does not visit the sick causes the person to die." For all I knew, simply the sound of another person in the room was something that she needed. Even the most tangential of relationships might be important.

She lived for a few more weeks. When she died, I wished her "Shabbat *shalom*."

Be Someone Else's Angel

It has been taught that Abraham circumcised himself at God's command and that God appeared to him as he was recovering. The Rabbis draw out this illustration by saying that God also made the day very hot so there would not be any travelers about who would come to Abraham's tent to trouble him. Nevertheless, Abraham was so hospitable that he insisted on getting up and looking outside his tent to see whether there was anyone who needed help. We can imagine the members of Abraham's family, Sarah especially, surrounding Abraham as his caregivers and trying to get him to sit down and take it easy. It was most likely to no avail, for Abraham was a headstrong man.

The Torah responds to this situation by saying that Abraham "lifted his eyes and looked, and three men were standing right next to him" (Genesis 18:2). They appeared right by his bedside. Who were these strangers? The Talmud says they were the angels Michael, Raphael, and Gabriel. Michael announced the wonder of Sarah's pregnancy, Raphael came to heal Abraham from his surgery, and Gabriel appeared to overturn the city of Sodom (Babylonian Talmud, *Bava Metzia* 86b).

Again, we see that the Torah teaches that people are angels, and anyone today who visits the sick is like Raphael the healer.

We can have the privilege of playing the role of being a divine messenger in someone's life in a time of need. We do not have to be more than human to do so. We simply have to show up when we should.

There is another, hidden teaching in this story as well. Abraham was ready to run out the door in search of travelers in his fanaticism to help other people, despite Sarah's protests. To get up and do so would have risked serious injury. God tried to keep him in bed by making the day hot. Any reasonable person would have stayed put. But Abraham was not reasonable. He was sick, and he wanted desperately to feel normal and do the things he was accustomed to doing, such as waiting on guests.

To prevent him from hurting himself, the angels appeared right next to him so that he did not have to get up. All Abraham needed to do was lift his eyes upward.

As caregivers, we try to anticipate people's needs. We try to take care of them as best we can. Sometimes we have to keep them from hurting themselves. This is not out of any feeling of self-sabotage. It is simply frustration. Our true

> We can have the privilege of being a divine messenger in someone's life in a time of need.

task is to help them turn their gaze upward toward the things that give them hope, strength, and inspiration. An encouraging word can be very powerful.

One of the easiest things we can do when people become incapacitated is to surround them with pictures of loved ones. It can be a wonderful gift to ask them to recall the names of the people in the pictures, what they are like, or the stories behind the photographs. In allowing people to tell these stories, even if they are ones you have heard before, you give a gift. You can bring back loving memories. This can be incredibly healing.

If we look inside ourselves, we can ask: What would I want if I were in their place? What would help me? To whom would I turn in my time of need? What would I need to make it through one more day? Looking within, we might see reflected there the universal needs we all feel. Redirecting someone's gaze from misery to encouragement or from despair to the face of a loved one can bring courage and strength. And perhaps the face that they are looking forward to seeing is yours.

PART THREE

Gathering Around

Dealing with Family

Where Were You When Mom Got Sick?

Life-changing illness, disability, aging, and mental conditions are not just individual problems. They affect the family, and it is likely that family members become the foremost caregivers for a loved one. Family has claims and responsibilities toward each other. These are people we did not choose; we are born into this circle. Yet when someone in our family faces poor health, the entire family is challenged. It is impossible to talk about illness and not talk about our families.

The trauma of sickness, like all life-cycle events, is never neutral as to how a family thinks and feels about itself. A significant event such as a serious illness in the family—or a wedding, birth, or funeral, for that matter—always either pushes a family closer together or pulls it further apart. "Do you remember when Grandma got sick?" we might ask. "We really all came together and were there for each other." Likewise, we might recall, "Do you remember when Dad was diagnosed with cancer? So-and-so never called." All crises are tests of a family's feelings and responsibilities.

But families are messy things. Even in the Bible, we do not see many healthy families. Our biblical ancestors are not necessarily positive role models of how to be good spouses, parents, or siblings. We are confronted in the book of Genesis with Abraham's triangle of conflict with his wife, Sarah, and his handmaid, Hagar (Genesis 21). Abraham and Sarah's son, Isaac, grows up despite his father offering him as a sacrifice on a mountaintop (Genesis 22). Isaac marries Rebecca, but they each choose a different child as their favorite. Isaac favors Esau, and Rebecca favors Jacob (Genesis 25:28). Rather than work out their differences, they pit their children against each other. Jacob repeats this saga of favoritism with his children, singling out Joseph and sparking his other sons' jealousy and hatred (Genesis 37). It is a long history of conflict that we have inherited, dating back to ancient times.[1] We can only wonder how each of these characters must have reacted when another member of the family got sick and needed support.

> The Torah's ideals of how family members should treat each other give us guideposts as we struggle to create life-affirming and balanced families, especially when facing a trauma such as illness.

Fortunately, conflict is not the only inheritance our ancestors have left us. The Hebrew Bible tells us of love and empathy. We read how Abraham grieved and took care of burying his wife (Genesis 23:2), how Rebecca showed kindness and devotion (Genesis 24:18–20), and how passionately Jacob loved Rachel (Genesis 29:11). We read of brotherly bonds and how we grow, discovering that our sibling rivals might become our best friends in adulthood (Genesis 45:1–7). Most of all, the Torah gives us commandments describing ideals of how family members should treat each other. These commandments, elaborated upon by the Sages, give us guideposts as we all struggle to create life-affirming and balanced families, especially when facing a trauma such as illness. In asking ourselves about physical and emotional health, we can refer to their wisdom to make sure that our families are systems of support.

What Are My
Obligations, and
What Are
My Limits?

Some of the most famous precepts about healthy family life are directed toward parents. Whenever we struggle with issues of how to deal with Dad when he can no longer drive, or how to help Mom with her medication, we can think of these passages from tradition.

HONORING AND REVERING OUR PARENTS

The Torah tells us two ideas concerning parents. On the one hand, it tells us to "honor your father and your mother" as one of the Ten Commandments (Exodus 20:12). On the other, the Torah says that we should "revere your mother and your father" (Leviticus 19:3). Both of these statements imply that we should respect our parents and care for their dignity and health. The Sages did not consider it an accident that the order of "father and mother" and "mother and father" is reversed in these two passages. They taught that the Torah tries to compensate for natural inclinations. The Sages felt that people often want to honor their mothers more than their fathers because mothers are usually more open to talking, and so the Torah asks us to honor our fathers first to make up for this imbalance. Likewise, we often show reverence or fear of our fathers more readily than our mothers, because the father is traditionally cast in the role of disciplinarian. Therefore, the Torah demands that we revere our mothers before our fathers. In this way, the Torah tries to teach equality in our attitude toward parents (*Mishnah Keritot* 6:9; *Shulchan Aruch, Yoreh Deah* 240).

What does "honoring" and "revering" your parents actually mean? The Rabbis simplify these values into concrete tasks. "Honoring," for the Rabbis, at minimum means that we provide them with food and drink, that we give them clothes and footwear, and that we make sure they can come and go. In other words, on a very basic level, we must take care of their needs in their old age. "Revering" has more to do with their dignity. We are not to stand or sit in their place at the table, we are not to openly contradict or embarrass them, and we are not to side with others against them. This even goes so far that if they behave badly and publicly insult you, you may not humiliate them in return (Babylonian Talmud, *Kiddushin* 31b; *Shulchan Aruch, Yoreh Deah* 240:2–4).

The Rabbis do not mention love in any of these passages. Although elsewhere they go on at length about love and affection by sons and daughters, here the Sages address a worst-case scenario in providing guidelines for a minimum amount of care. Even if a relationship with a father or mother is full of conflict, it is still possible to fulfill the obligations of "honoring" and "revering." As one human being to another, we are obligated to take care of our parents' basic physical needs in their old age. When even these basic tasks are difficult to do, if we can resist showing disrespect to them, we keep from lowering ourselves to behavior that is beneath us. The Rabbis sought to guarantee humane treatment for the elderly and also, no matter what our personal history, that we should always strive to be good people.

It is also inspiring when a loved one goes "beyond the call of duty." Thankfully, most of us love our parents and gladly and willingly would sacrifice what we need to for them. One man I know, however, did not have any children. In his old age, Bill's niece stepped in and was there for him just like a loving daughter. Although she lived out of town, she called and visited regularly, made sure he received the best possible care, and informed all of Bill's friends about how things were going. Even though this man endured a long series of hospitalizations, his niece's love and loyalty never wavered. She spoke sensitively to him and listened respectfully to how her uncle felt. In the end, Bill's niece took care of him in ways that many children do not live up to. She enabled her uncle to live out his last days in as much dignity and comfort as possible, even facing the difficult challenge of whether or not to insist to her uncle that he go into a nursing home. Bill died before that had to happen.

> When dealing with family, push with the left hand and draw near with the right.
>
> *KITZUR SHULCHAN*
> *ARUCH* 165:7

GUARDING OUR PARENTS' SAFETY

It may be comforting to know that the emotional dilemma of putting a parent in an assisted living or nursing home is centuries old, and just as we agonize over the decision, so did those who came before us. Too often, the only time we go into an assisted living or nursing home facility is when we have a crisis. A parent falls, and living at home is no longer an option. This causes a great deal of panic and last-minute decision making. Even when we are positive we are doing the right thing, we still feel guilty because we are the ones who appear to be taking away our loved one's independence.

In truth it is their ill health that has taken away their independence. We are acting to protect their safety and the safety of others. This case is most urgently manifest when the beloved mother or father has dementia or some other mental incapacity and cannot understand why you are putting her or him in a home. Even the most loving parents can heap abuse upon their children when they do not understand and resent the situation. Nevertheless, we are bound to do the right thing for our parents and their health, even if they fight us. It was none other than Moses Maimonides, a great Jewish physician and philosopher, who wrote:

> If one's father or mother is mentally incapacitated, one should endeavor to engage with them as much as they are able until God has mercy on them. If it is impossible and one finds oneself in extreme anguish, one may leave them and go to others and delegate them to take care of them as they need.
>
> MISHNEH TORAH, LAWS OF REBELS 6:7

Often, a long-term care facility is the only option to provide appropriate care for our parents or grandparents. This passage also addresses the excruciating challenge of when we have to institutionalize someone such as, God forbid, a child or a spouse. These moments are ones of anguish and guilt. You might ask yourself, "How can I leave him in a place like that?"

The Sages respond by saying that there is nothing immoral about taking these measures if they are done with honor and reverence and are performed truly in the sick person's best interest.

STRIVING FOR BALANCE IN OUR RELATIONSHIPS

Just as the duties to our parents have requirements but boundaries, so too can the same be said for parents toward children. In ancient times the father was the key provider of a family, but we can understand that the obligations in Jewish law of a father toward his children pertain to both parents in contemporary times. According to Jewish law, even in a conflicted family, parents are obligated to perform the Jewish rituals welcoming a child into the covenant of Abraham and Sarah, teach them Torah, teach them a craft, and enable them to get married (Babylonian Talmud, *Kiddushin* 29b). Further, there are things parents may not do. They may not impose too heavy a burden upon their children, they may never beat their children, and they may never ask their children to do anything immoral that the Torah would condemn. Not only that, but if the parents give up their honor by enjoying a relaxed or jesting moment, they cannot suddenly demand it back; parents owe their children consistency (*Shulchan Aruch, Yoreh Deah* 240:15, 19, 20).

What is clear from these duties and obligations is that Jewish tradition has no room for any kind of abuse or neglect. Even outside of extreme circumstances, both parents and children are to be respected as individuals even as we are obligated to be involved in each other's lives. We balance what we must do for our loved ones and insist on our involvement, but at the same time we are not given permission to rule over them and entangle ourselves in ways that are invasive or disrespectful. Health can only come with balance.

Preserving Respect and Dignity

Similar claims are also made in Judaism regarding a person's husband or wife. As early as the story of Adam and Eve, we learn that we all seek out a partner who helps us and completes us. The Torah tells us that God created Eve from Adam. Adam and Eve were once one person until God divided them (Genesis 2:18–24). We pursue a feeling of that wholeness and unity when seeking out our life's partner.

It is instructive, however, that once Adam and Eve found each other, they did not merge back into one. They remained two distinct individuals. In fact, the Torah describes Eve's relationship with Adam in very specific words. She is called "a help to match him" (Genesis 2:18). Jewish tradition understands that this means that each partner has an equal role to play and equally worthy needs to be met. If they are worthy, they will be a "help" to each other, and when they fail in these ideals, they are obligated to challenge each other in a "match," demanding that the other show the respect that they ought (Rashi on Genesis 2:18, from Babylonian Talmud, *Yevamot* 63a).

It therefore became institutionalized in Jewish tradition that each partner in a marriage is owed not only care and support but also respect and dignity. The love of a couple is built on such a foundation. Many of these ideals were written into the *ketubah*, the prenuptial agreement that a Jewish couple signs before their wedding. Ideally, the marriage is one of two equal individuals, balancing love and involvement with individual space and desires. Nothing, of course, tests these boundaries like illness.

Let us consider a couple named Sol and Helen. Helen was diagnosed with Alzheimer's disease. Sol took care of her himself in their home for six years. He fed her, clothed her, and bathed her. He talked to her every day, and he read the newspaper to her. After six years, he admitted her into a nursing home. Her condition had progressed to the point where he was not able to take care of her anymore, and he was becoming ill himself because of the stress of the situation.

Upon visiting with both of them in the care facility, I could only get a glimpse of the emotional hardship Sol faced. The conversation went something like this:

> "Where am I?" Helen asked.
>
> "This is where you live, dear," Sol answered.
>
> "I live here?"
>
> "Yes, dear."
>
> "Why do I live here? Why aren't I at home?" she asked with clear pain in her voice.
>
> "Now, honey, we talked about this. I couldn't take care of you anymore, so this is the place where you can be safe and taken care of."
>
> "Where am I?" she asked again.
>
> "This is where you live, dear."
>
> "Why do I live here? Why am I not home with you?"

And so the conversation repeated, demanding endless patience and calm. Nevertheless, Sol held his ground. He started coming to classes and activities at the synagogue for the first time in years, and in his own words, he began "to live again." He did not regret a moment of care he gave to his wife. He just refused to stop living and annihilate himself for her.

Similarly, another man lost his job because of an injury. Richard's lower back could not stand to do the labor that he once did. In addition, he developed a heart condition that made any kind of strain dangerous.

His marriage was a traditional one. His wife, Rebecca, took care of all the domestic chores. She cooked, did the laundry and the dishes, and maintained a house that was spotless. Richard's role was as a provider, but his loss of health devastated his self-image.

Part of what made their marriage work was that they each had individual lives and time away from each other during the day. Now that had vanished. As Richard spent more time at home, he became more and more helpless. Whereas Rebecca was used to being able to go out during the day, she now felt equally trapped at home, catering to her husband's needs. "I can't leave him," she would say.

Rebecca's friends kept saying to her that she needed to get out of the house for her own sanity. One friend invited her to come work with her in her store selling stationery, invitations, and other customized paper products. After several weeks, Rebecca accepted. It was only part time, but it was still a bold move for her. She didn't need the money, although the extra income was nice. She simply needed something in her life to call her own. The first week on the job, her husband fell on the stairs leading up to the house. He asked that she quit. She resolutely said no.

Her insistence most likely saved their marriage. It was also not too long after that that Richard learned to use the microwave oven. He found new interests and projects for himself.

Dealing with family in moments of trial can be like a tug-of-war. There is a push and pull as we try to do our best and leave the rest up to God. Jewish law puts it this way: "When dealing with family, push with the left hand and draw near with the right" (*Kitzur Shulchan Aruch* 165:7).

Too Close for Comfort

The commandments from the Rabbis about obligations of parents to children, children to parents, and spouses to each other provoke some questions: What role do relationships play in the process of healing? Which relationships can be helpful? Which relationships are inappropriate?

There is wisdom in the practice that family serve as caregivers, but there is a line that should not be crossed. Most obviously, surgeons will not operate on their spouses, nor can psychologists accept their children or parents as patients. Similarly, it would be inappropriate for patients to also play the role of their own doctor. Doctors know that they are the worst patients, mainly because they think they know better. We need professionals in the process of healing not only because of their expertise but also because we lose all objectivity when we evaluate and help ourselves. There is such a thing as a healthy distance between the ill and the caregiver. Sometimes we can be too close to the subject to have a balanced approach to what is right and wrong. The problem is not a lack of caring. The problem is actually the opposite. It is too much closeness. Although we might be accustomed to thinking that intimacy is positive and helpful, it can also be a hindrance.

The Torah also implies this principle of a healthy distance when it talks about Adam and Eve. As mentioned earlier, Adam and Eve began as one, but they do not become one again. They remain two distinct individuals. Yet too often, in caring for another, we become enmeshed in the other person's life to our detriment.

Sarah, for instance, found herself facing a crisis. She worked as a secretary at a local business. Her husband developed a neurological condition and was soon unable to work. She was unwilling to accept this change in their lives, and she did not like to talk about it. She would go from her demanding job to an even more demanding situation at home. Finances also became a problem.

After some time, Sarah herself began to show physical symptoms of stress. She felt out of control and constantly on the verge of panic. Rather than turning to others for help to deal with her anxiety, Sarah began taking "organic remedies," that is, "all natural" drugs available without a prescription (and also without governmental regulation), to help her deal with her anxiety.

As her husband's condition worsened, Sarah continued to keep her problems bottled up inside. "I know what is best for us," she would insist. She was on her way to killing herself from stress and exhaustion when her husband passed away. The couple's children confessed to me that they felt their father's death merciful, for with their father's death their mother's life was saved.

Sarah's life was so enmeshed in her husband's that she almost killed herself. She also forgot about her children and grandchildren, who also needed her. One can only wonder how different this story might have been if she had turned and asked for help, both for her husband and for herself.

Regular visits from a friend, an appeal to her boss at work, or simply talking about how she was feeling with a member of the clergy, a social worker, or a psychologist might have prevented Sarah from making herself ill along with her husband.

Healthy families manage a kind of balancing act that involves acknowledging distance between people, even lovers. The members of the family are connected to each other through love and empathy. They are involved in each other's lives and genuinely care for and need each other. At the same time, the members of the family are not enmeshed in each other. They are responsible for their own lives and are free to pursue their individual aspirations. The members of a healthy family are not distant or cut off from each other, nor are they overly involved or suffocating. The healthy family has a healthy balance of connectedness and individuation.

> The Golden Rule is "Love your neighbor as yourself" (Leviticus 19:18). Perhaps a variation on it should be "Love another and yourself."

The healthy family also shows a balance when it comes to accomplishing tasks and meeting life's challenges. Somewhere between rigid discipline and complete chaos, a healthy family shows flexibility. The family has a plan and goals for the future, but when things go awry or change comes unexpectedly, the family is able to adjust with a minimal amount of panic.[2]

In other words, the members of a healthy family are able to say, "I am responsible for those in my family, but I am responsible for myself first. Here is where I end and you begin."

Allow me to tell you about a couple I will never forget who epitomized the worst form of enmeshment. They lived in Florida.

Hyman and Esther were in a terrible car accident. In this horrible wreck, both of these elderly people became crippled. They required full-time help to stay with them in their home, twenty-four hours a day. At least, their caretakers thought, they could suffer through this tragedy together in the comfort of their own home.

The couple, it turns out, were Holocaust survivors. They had both been deported to concentration camps in Europe as Jews singled out by Adolf Hitler to die a dehumanizing death. Having survived this unimaginable ordeal, the two met at a displaced persons' camp. They came to the United States, married, and raised a family. Unlike some survivors, they were both very reluctant to talk about their experience, even with their children. Nevertheless, having now become victims of this new catastrophe in their old age, Esther described the car accident as her "second Holocaust."

In my visits to this couple, I would take each one out in a wheelchair separately to stroll on the sidewalk of their street. In doing so, I uncovered a secret that was at the heart of their suffering. The tragedy in this house with two hospital beds contained layer after layer. These people had endured the Holocaust and should not have had to endure any more suffering. Now they had become crippled. At least, one might think, they still had each other.

Esther and Hyman each confessed to me during my time alone with them individually that the worst part of their suffering was not their memories of the Holocaust or that they were now crippled. The worst part of their suffering was that they had a miserable marriage. They had stayed together because they felt that divorce was a stigma, especially for a couple of Holocaust survivors. In their minds, to get a divorce would have been an unbearable act of shame. Over the years, their relationship had deteriorated to the point where they could not speak a peaceful word to one another.

The real tragedy of their accident was that, partly by reason of the accident and partly because of their own sense of pride and shame, this couple was now forced to spend every moment of every day in each other's presence. Only when people from the outside came in and took them out of the house were they relieved of the greatest source of their suffering. Their backaches and bedsores were nothing compared to the spiritual destruction of their marriage and their current imprisonment. Their inability to walk paled in comparison to their inability to escape from each other.

These extreme situations should serve as a warning. We must nurture ourselves so that when our closest loved ones cannot be there for us we are not lost to life. We are not to martyr ourselves on their behalf. We also need to remember that the people with whom we enmesh our lives are the people with whom we will grow old. They will be the spouses or children who are supposed to take care of us and see us when we are at our worst. They will be the ones who come (or don't come) when we are sick. We must therefore nurture loving relationships as best we can, seek counseling and therapy when things go awry, and have faith that love will be reciprocated.

The Golden Rule is "Love your neighbor as yourself" (Leviticus 19:18). Perhaps a variation on it should be "Love another and yourself."

Who Is Sick?

Amother calls me about her only child, who is away at college. Evan is having a rough time. He was always an earnest and sensitive person, and my interaction with him at the synagogue was always positive. He always brought candy to class and handed it out not only to his friends but also to anyone who wanted some. When his parents asked me to write him a recommendation for college, I accepted gladly and wrote a glowing letter.

Once at college, Evan did not thrive. He complained of migraine headaches with pain so debilitating that he would become nauseated. Although medication helped, the headaches kept recurring. While in class, he often had trouble concentrating, and he would sleep late into the morning. At a college dormitory, this was not unusual because most students stayed up very late and then slept in, taking their classes in the afternoon. It took a while for his roommate to realize that Evan was not just sleeping late but sleeping all the time, and when he was up he would complain of a headache. Evan failed most of his first-semester classes.

Evan's parents were in a panic. What was wrong with Evan? Doctors hypothesized about the change in climate and the pressure that this put on his sinuses. Maybe he was simply a bad student. But why was he sleeping so much? Why was Evan behaving this way?

After a few discussions with Evan's parents, it became clear that Evan was only part of the picture. Evan was diagnosed with depression coupled with chronic anxiety, and thankfully, today both of these diseases are highly treatable. Unfortunately, many such cases go undiagnosed, and people suffer and become even more ill. But Evan's depression and anxiety did not happen in a vacuum. Although he was ultimately responsible for his own life, how he got to this state had more to do with what was going on at home than with what was going on at college.

Evan's parents had always had marital difficulties. There was always a great deal of tension in the house, and at some point during his years growing up, Evan's father and mother had stopped talking to each other in any kind of emotional fashion. In Evan's early adolescence, his parents had considered divorce, but they decided it was better to stay together for Evan's sake. Evan's leaving the house for college had caused a family crisis. What would happen now?

> Sometimes the person who is visibly ill is not the only one who is sick.

Evan had come to understand his role as the keeper of the family peace. In his family, Evan's presence in the home made for his parents' sense of stability. It was stability, however, with chronic anxiety. Even though he could not express it, Evan felt responsible for his parents' marriage.

This does not happen to all families where there is a bad marriage in the home. This is also not the only reason why people suffer from depression or anxiety disorders. And some kids have a hard time going away to college. This was simply the problem as it manifested itself in this family. As soon as

Evan's parents entered marital counseling and began to take responsibility for their own relationship, Evan found that he could study while away at school.

Rabbi Edwin H. Friedman was one of the pioneers of thinking about the family in the context of healing. Among other things, he articulated a way of thinking about illness that takes into account the importance of family. This might seem self-evident to some, but it may be disturbing to others. We are used to thinking of the Jewish family seated around the Passover holiday table, with everyone smiling and singing and enjoying matzah ball soup.

Families, however, are more than just this idyllic picture. Jewish families are just as subject to illness, including substance abuse and mental illness, as all other families. When someone becomes ill, it is incumbent upon us to ask whether the pressures and position within the family may be a contributing factor.

When someone walks into the doctor's office, that person takes on the role of the patient. That person may, however, represent a deeper malady in the set of relationships that is in the family. In Rabbi Friedman's words:

> The concept of the identified patient ... is that the family member with the obvious symptom is to be seen not as the "sick one" but as the one in whom the family's stress or pathology has surfaced.... Physicians obviously do not assume that the part of a human organism that is in pain, or failing to function properly, is necessarily the cause of its own distress. The color of the skin can be related to a problem in the liver; a pain in the jaw could be referred from angina. And so it is ... with the organism known as the human family.... In a child it could take the form of excessive bedwetting, hyperactivity, school failures, drugs,

obesity, or juvenile diabetes; in a spouse its form could be excessive drinking, depression, chronic ailments, a heart condition, or perhaps even cancer; in an aged member of the family it could show up as confusion, senility, or agitated and random behavior.[3]

The role of family is critical when facing illness. A person's sickness may be a manifestation of the dysfunction of a family, and the identified patient is the only one showing it. Like a water pipe that is under too much pressure, eventually one joint is going to burst. It does not mean that joint is bad. It means that there was too much pressure in the whole pipe to begin with.

In other words, when someone is ill, it is a mistake to look at that person in isolation. Our family can serve as support but can also contribute to pain. Sometimes a person's relationships can be the cause of the illness in the first place. Sometimes the person who is visibly ill is not the only one who is sick. The whole family might be sick, and it is only one person who is showing the symptoms and taking responsibility for the illness. What stress or anxiety might a person be carrying for the whole family?

Taking responsibility for ourselves as a family means being open to the possibility that we have to talk about our family issues and examine how one person's behavior affects others. Often a rabbi or other figure can help recommend a good counselor or therapist to help on this path. Even if we feel shame or guilt, we should also feel a sense of obligation that we need to pursue health together, as the imperative calls to us, "Choose life, so that you and your children may live" (Deuteronomy 30:19).

The Meaning of *Shalom Bayit* (Peace in the Home)

When facing illness, families are forced to spend a great deal of time together. Sometimes people who are estranged find themselves with each other for long periods of time. This increased presence sometimes makes it harder to suppress annoyances, disappointments, judgments, and opinions about others that we would usually keep to ourselves. It takes a great deal of effort to say, "I am here for so-and-so's sake, and I am not going to let that person get in the way of my visit."

There is a Hebrew phrase in Judaism that means "peace in one's house." It is *shalom bayit*. *Shalom* means "peace" or "wholeness," and *bayit* means "home" or "house." We are all asked to strive for peace in our homes. We are all asked to make sacrifices for the sake of family peace. But *shalom bayit* does not really mean that our house is a tranquil or calm place. It does not mean an absence of conflict. Rather, the phrase *shalom bayit* is used in the sense of "I could have said something, but I kept silent for the sake of *shalom bayit*." Or "I didn't want to spend the holidays with them, but I went for *shalom bayit*."

Shalom bayit, peace in the home, does not really have to do with the level of noise and the order of things in your house. Instead, this kind of *shalom* has more to do with compromise. In your family, there is probably at least one person who knows how to "push your buttons" or get a rise out of you. These family members know just what to say and how and when to say it to get you to react and behave badly. When the family is under the strains of illness, this reaction may be easier to achieve.

> *Shalom bayit* really means the "acceptance of family."

It is a waste of your energy to try to change these family members. You may want to make them into the people you would rather they be. You might rail against parents, children, or siblings, wishing they were more like the imaginary figures you hold in your fantasies or the partner or loved one you wish you had. It is easy to be bitter when your loved ones do not live up to your expectations.

In light of this and our understanding of healing, perhaps in this context *shalom* is more in line with the meaning of "acceptance" than anything else. Married or single, with or without children, we all belong to families. Can you accept others for who they are with all of their imperfections, or will you continue to fight against their identity and habits to try to change them into the people you would like them to be? Are you going to drive yourself crazy about a family dispute from perhaps decades ago, or are you going to compromise and let your family be your family? And will you be humble enough to remember that they might be trying to accept you as well?

Shalom bayit, peace in the home, really means the "acceptance of family." Nothing tries a family more than illness. We are called upon to serve others in whom we may be disappointed. Perhaps our disappointment also needs evaluation. *Shalom bayit* does not mean that we have to stop being who we are; it does mean that we have to stop demanding that others be something different from who they are. Respecting ourselves and respecting others ultimately lead to balance and health, especially when faced with trial.

When We Cry
Out of Love

In the Torah, we are witness to a terrible fight within a family. Moses and his sister Miriam and his brother Aaron have an all-out war with each other about Moses's wife. The details are not important. What is important is what happens next.

After the fight, Miriam becomes afflicted with a terrible disease. Aaron sees Miriam's affliction and describes it graphically:

> Let her not be like someone who is dead, who came out of the mother's womb with half of her flesh eaten away!
>
> NUMBERS 12:12

Miriam looks gruesome. We can imagine that her brothers think, "Can this be my sister?" All arguing suddenly stops. There is more important business at hand. They stand in shock at their sister's suffering.

Their experience is not unique. There are times when we see our loved ones with afflictions or taking treatments that change their appearance. Sometimes, when our loved ones die, we protect our children from seeing them because we do not want them to be remembered looking that way.

Moses cries out on behalf of his sister: "Please, God, heal her!" (Numbers 12:13). It is the shortest prayer in the Torah but also full of anguish. In Hebrew, the verse reads in poetic rhyme, *El na r'fa na lah!* These are the same syllables of the name of the healing angel Raphael, only in a different order. Moses invokes God's power of healing in his time of need.

God responds, and Miriam heals after seven days. The Torah also says that her family and the rest of the Israelite people would not break camp and move forward without her. They wait until she is with them before setting out. No one would leave her behind.

Moses's love for his sister was intense. The same intensity that led to their argument also is contained in Moses's outburst to God. We can also imagine that her love was the same for him. Their family was full of deep emotion that sometimes came out violently toward one another but also formed bonds of devotion in the face of adversity.

Our love in our families is similar. That intensity, for good and for bad, is part of the passion of what it means to be a family. Our families form the arena where most of us work out our lives. We bruise each other, and we also stand by each other. When one of us suffers, we all suffer.

> Our families form the arena where most of us work out our lives. We bruise each other, and we also stand by each other.

Perhaps we should also learn to be gentle with each other. Our plea to God is like our cry to our family when we are in need:

> For You, Sovereign, are good and forgiving,
> Full of love....
> In my distress, I will call You
> For You will answer me.
>
> Psalm 86:5, 86:7

PART FOUR

Reaching Upward

Searching for God

Why Praying Can Help Even If You've Never Done It Before

When facing illness, whether in our own life or the life of another, the greatest spiritual tool at our disposal is prayer. It is a tool that is not used often enough, however, because many people are uncomfortable with the idea. "I'm just not the praying type," we might say.

Despite our reservations, prayer appears to be a human need. It is a natural thing for people to worship in some fashion. Although I know of no scientific study, I would bet that the act of prayer is and has been a part of every culture in the world throughout history. Despite this natural inclination, modern men and women often find it difficult or awkward to pray. They feel embarrassed or self-conscious. Perhaps it is the feeling of being ignorant of or estranged from religious ritual or language. Perhaps it is the direct way prayer asks us to display emotion. Perhaps it is simply something that we never did growing up or never saw our parents do.

Nevertheless, we sometimes pray, despite ourselves. When we exhale in relief that a danger has passed us by, when we stumble for words to show our amazement at a landscape, or when we put our hands over our hearts and invoke God to keep our country safe, whether we realize it or not, we are praying.

Certainly when we face illness, religion naturally presents itself, whether from a concerned loved one or a neighbor, a chaplain dropping by, or a religious symbol in a hospital.

Prayer is simply talking to God, either out loud with our mouths or silently in our heads. Prayer is an expression of the soul, and it does not much matter what form that expression takes.

> Prayer is an expression of the soul, and it does not much matter what form that expression takes.

Psychologists and other professionals have long understood the value of simply talking, of trying to articulate thoughts and emotions. There is therapeutic value in telling personal stories, letting out feelings, and knowing that there is a listening ear. Perhaps we might grow in maturity and self-awareness as a result.

Talking to God, however, implies all of this and more. In addition to the benefits of expressing your feelings, you also acknowledge and address something larger than yourself that puts your life in perspective. Praying is, by its very nature, an unequal conversation. You as a speaker pray to a greater listener. By praying, you do more than talk. You let yourself enter into a relationship where you are the smaller party. Your pain, your challenges, and your growth are put up against that larger universe and the Source from which we all come.

In a way, by praying, you "decentralize" yourself. Much of the time, it is natural to think of yourself as the center of your own universe. We are all preoccupied with our problems, made ever more real by our suffering. We can even sulk and stew. By praying, however, you willingly take yourself out of the middle and acknowledge that there is an Other who is present at all times, the true center of existence. Rather than the planets, sun, moon, and stars revolving around you, you acknowledge that you are the one who revolves around God.

A woman recently told me of a plaque that she has in her office that reads, "Please retire from being the CEO of the universe." We do not have to understand everything, fix everything, and control everything. We just have to respond to life in a way that is fitting in the eyes of God.

Where Did All These Prayers Come From?

The link between religion and medicine goes back thousands of years, and many of the hospitals in the world were founded by religious orders. The names of our hospitals often show their religious roots, such as Holy Cross or Mount Sinai. Hospitals are also named for saints or denominations. Even in cultures that are not Christian or Jewish, figures such as shamans or "medicine men" illustrate the link between religion and medicine. There is something awe inspiring about healing that brings out notions of the Divine in much of humanity.

Considering prayer in this light, it might not seem so strange or awkward to connect prayer with healing. Prayer has a long history in Judaism, and there are many examples that can serve as our guides. In Scripture and other sacred literature, people recorded their conversations with God; through these conversations we can explore what other people's problems and prayers have meant over time.

Certainly we find many of the people in the Hebrew Bible talking to God. Abraham, Sarah, Moses, and others talk constantly to God. Out of all these characters from all the biblical stories, the one figure who became a paradigm in Judaism of how to pray is a woman named Hannah.

When the Rabbis of antiquity were looking for a role model to imitate in prayer, they turned to the opening chapter of the book of Samuel and found Hannah. Hannah faced the ancient and devastating problem of infertility. She found relief from her pain by talking to God: "Hannah was praying with her heart; while her lips were moving, her voice could not be heard" (1 Samuel 1:13). In fact, Hannah was so lost in the expression of her heart that an outside observer mistook the situation and thought she was drunk. When she finished her prayers, we read that she rose from her conversation with

> Prayer is about forgetting what you look like and doing what you need to do.

God feeling some sense of relief. "The woman went on her way, she ate, and her face was no longer dejected" (1 Samuel 1:18).

To this day, a common Jewish posture of prayer is reading from a siddur, the traditional prayer book, so that a person's lips move but the voice is silent. You might see people in synagogues swaying while praying or humming Hebrew words of a prayer to themselves. For many, this traditional davening or praying in imitation of Hannah simply "feels right" in an inexplicable way. Prayer, however, is not limited to this one posture.

What is perhaps most important to learn from Hannah is that she clearly did not feel self-conscious while she was praying. She was not concerned about how she looked or sounded. She simply prayed, even if she looked strange to an outside observer. For modern people, this may be the biggest gap between how Hannah prayed and what happens when we try to pray. Our words get stuck and our minds freeze because we are worried about what other people will think of us.

Hannah teaches us that prayer is about forgetting what you look like and doing what you need to do. You might need to give God "a good talking to." You might even need to yell and be angry; it's okay, because God can take it. It might even feel somewhat self-indulgent to talk about yourself in this way. Remember Rabbi Nachman of Breslov encouraging us to break through this barrier and talk to God the way a child has a heart-to-heart talk with a father or mother. Your problems become shared as you enter into a relationship. You stop trying to hold up our entire world and let God in to listen and help. You can forget what the person is doing in front of you, beside you, or in back of you and simply take your own private moment to think your words to God.

Hannah's prayer gave her relief. It "worked" for her because she prayed from the heart. Later rabbis echo this need to speak from the heart in order for prayer to alleviate stress and give us some kind of peace of mind.

In ancient times, worship took the form of sacrifices. A man or woman would offer up an animal and then serve it as food for his or her family, the servants of the Temple in Jerusalem, and God. This form of prayer literally provided sustenance. The mysteries of life and death, the act of eating something killed in order to live, and the burning smoke and incense drew powerful emotions from the worshiper. The Hebrew word for "sacrifice" is *korban*. The letters at the root of this word are *k-r-v*, which is also the root of the Hebrew verb "to draw close." A person literally drew close to God through sacrifice.

By the time the Temple was destroyed by conquerors, people had already begun to change their mode of worship. Prayer replaced sacrifice, but the idea of offering something up, even something painful, and thereby drawing close to God, remained central to Jewish life and thought. Prayer, therefore, had to be from the heart. It had to truly mean something, even if it involved some degree of painful revelation. Prayer had to be a kind of sacrifice.

It is for this reason that the Rabbis call prayer the "service of the heart" (Babylonian Talmud, *Ta'anit* 2a). No matter what the posture of prayer, it must be heartfelt. One powerful image that the Rabbis offer illustrates what they meant by heartfelt prayer: on Yom Kippur, the Day of Atonement, fasting was supposed to help amplify how heartfelt a prayer was, so much so that the prayer leader would exhort the worshipers, "Let us raise our hearts in our hands" (Babylonian Talmud, *Ta'anit* 8a on Lamentations 3:41). It has thus been true in Judaism that without the heart, prayers are only words. We must be willing to have our hearts in our hands and raise them up to God.

Today, we may not attend prayer services at synagogue often, and we may feel awkward about prayer in general. Indeed, the Sages argue whether or not "the gates of prayer" are always open (Lamentations Rabbah 3:44). Some feel that they are sometimes closed in that certain people cannot break through their personal barriers and pray, yet other Rabbis claim that the gates of prayer are never locked. The power of prayer, however, is often not manifest in how frequently or fluently you say a prayer (although familiarity can make you feel less self-conscious). Rather, the main thing is how deeply you mean it when you say it. The depth of a prayer in your heart gives light to the meaning of the prayer in your life.

Grown-up Prayer

Can you remember when you prayed for something when you were a child? For what did you pray?

The main reason most of us prayed when we were children was to petition God for something. "Please, please, please can I just have....," we begged. Perhaps we prayed for a new toy, a new bicycle, or a good grade on a test. We asked for magic to work just for us. We wanted special effects that catered to our needs. We might even have dreamt and thought it was possible that if we hoped hard enough, the world would oblige. We prayed for miracle cures and divine intervention. The psychologist Sigmund Freud called this "wish fulfillment."[1]

As we grow and mature, however, hopefully we stop praying for physical changes in the laws of nature and start praying for internal changes within ourselves. Prayers we say as children differ from the prayers we say as adults. We learn to pray for intangible things such as patience, tranquility, or strength. We pray for the courage to face changes and transitions in our lives. We pray for the willingness to apologize to or forgive another. As we age, we petition God for equanimity, fortitude, and peace of mind. These are reasons why adults pray, and these are vital resources for healing.

Just as we pray to say "please," we also pray to say "thank you." We express our gratitude in prayer. When a baby is born, whom shall we thank? When we witness a milestone in a grand-child's life, how else are we to show our appreciation? Showing our gratitude for the miracles that occur in our everyday lives moves us to prayer. Illness or aging may move us to say thank you more often. Each day becomes more precious as it slips by.

Finally, in our older years as we mature even further, we find ourselves praying to express awe. When people praise God, they are showing their enormous wonder at the universe. To see starry skies, beautiful trees, or breathtaking canyons makes us instinctively want to praise the Creator. What happens inside of us is connected with the world outside. We realize that our finite bodies are part of it all. Everything has a beginning and an end, and we can no longer take things for granted. A woman in her nineties named Jenny once expressed it to me this way: "The years are so short, and the days are so long. It makes me pray every day."

Often, we do not have words to express what is going on in our hearts, and so, if we are comfortable with a religious tradition, we might turn to liturgical formulas to indicate something of what we are feeling. Using a symbolic language, such as Hebrew, lets us point beyond the words to something that transcends us.

And sometimes, all we can do is be silent in complete awe and wonder. The Jewish philosopher Moses Maimonides felt that silence was the best form of prayer because silence does not try to pin God down to specific words but simply acknowledges the mystery in which we all find ourselves. He quotes Psalms: "For You, silence is praise" (*Guide of the Perplexed* 1:59, on Psalm 65:2).[2]

Being aware of why we pray can be important when it comes to facing illness and using prayer as a tool of comfort. We have to be aware of what distinguishes childhood prayer from the prayer of an adult. If we are stuck back in our childhood mode of prayer, of praying for the laws of nature to reverse themselves just for our sake, not to fix a bicycle but to fix a loved one, not to give us a good grade but to give us a good doctor's report, not to beat up bullies but to beat up cancer, then we are engaging in the kind of wishful thinking that often sets us up for disappointment. Prayer is different from magic in that it is about internal change in our souls in relation to God and not about external change through supernatural miracles.

> By directing us inward, prayer can make us appreciate the regular, everyday occurrences that are miracles we often overlook.

This does not mean that we cannot express our hopes in the form of prayers, even if we know that our hopes are unrealistic. Prayer can help us define what we want versus what is real. "I wish I did not have to go through this," is a very common prayer. Although the Hebrew word *l'hitpalel* is understood in Judaism to mean "to pray," it is also a reflexive verb that might be understood as meaning "to reflect on oneself." Prayer can express our hopes, but it is also a reality test for what kind of change the world permits.

By directing us inward, prayer at its best can make us appreciate not the extraordinary events, such as splitting seas or rare recoveries, but the regular, everyday occurrences that are miracles we often overlook. Jewish prayer asks us to find the extraordinary within the ordinary. We are asked to say prayers over simple loaves of bread, cups of wine, and the washing of hands. We are told to say prayers over our children and our elders. We pray in appreciation for the ability to go to sleep each night and get up each morning.

What Prayer
Cannot Do

There has been a great deal of controversy during the past two decades about the power of prayer in relation to healing. Prayer is known to reduce stress and increase hope, which can improve health. People who pray regularly and take care of themselves spiritually and psychologically live healthier lives.

But there have always been those who have claimed that through supernatural intervention, a heartfelt prayer alone cured a disease. There have also been reports about "remote healing," where someone in another room or even another country prays for someone else, with noticeable physical results. As reported by ABC News in August 2001, some doctors at the Mid America Heart Institute in Kansas City have tried to conduct experiments to see whether "remote healing" is efficacious. Several of the doctors claimed that they witnessed miracles in which the patients who had people pray for them had better recoveries than those who did not have people pray for them.[3] One such famous study was conducted by Dr. Randolph Byrd in San Francisco, and several have been published in the *Annals of Internal Medicine* since then.

Although it is tempting to conclude from these studies that such kinds of prayer "work" in producing tangible results, a closer look at these studies reveals that they are all seriously flawed. There has not been a single study of "remote healing" or other such practices that has not been found to be lacking.[4] There is no proof at all that intercessory prayer results in supernatural healing.

Not only that, but fundamentally there is no study that could possibly prove such a claim because how a person evaluates healing and recovery scientifically is entirely different from how we evaluate prayer. Did the person pray with a certain amount of devotion? How often and how deeply did a person pray? How do you quantify it? Does a person's religion matter? A person's theology? These are questions that cannot be answered objectively.

> The true power of prayer is not manifest in supernatural wish fulfillment but in instilling within us humility and gratitude toward life, making it easier to cope.

A completely different story results, however, when we know another is praying for us and we have positive feelings about prayer. If there is a connection between a sick individual and a community, then prayer can be a tool that can reduce stress and help promote health. When we pray under these circumstances, we admit the truth that we do not have any control over disease other than our attitude and what the doctor prescribes. The true power of prayer is not manifest in supernatural wish fulfillment but in instilling within us humility and gratitude toward life, making it easier to cope. It is perhaps for this reason that Jewish law states, "Anyone who visits [the sick] and does not pray for him has not fulfilled his sacred obligation" (*Shulchan Aruch, Yoreh Deah* 335:5).

The true power of prayer is in feeling connected. By connecting one human being with another, and through that relationship being connected to God, we are able to have a helpful perspective when facing illness. Through moments of connection, we grow as human beings by learning to feel grateful and by being humble.

Why "We" Pray

Feeling connected to God is easier when we feel connected to each other and those who came before us. It is an important rule in Judaism that the ideal situation for prayer is to pray with others and not to pray alone. Even when we do pray alone, the traditional prayers are still said in the first person plural. The person standing alone says "we." We are to see ourselves as part of a larger group. "Do not separate yourself from the community," the sage Hillel said as early as the second century (*Pirkei Avot* 2:4). In Jewish prayers for healing, therefore, we always mention that a person should be healed "among all those others who are sick among the people Israel."

> ## Do not separate yourself from the community.
> *PIRKEI AVOT* 2:4

Originally, traditional Jewish prayers such as the prayer for healing referred to only the Jewish community, the "people Israel." The reason for this is that the original speakers of this prayer often found themselves in a hostile environment and had to stand in solidarity with other Jews. Today we are fortunate enough to expand our sense of community to a more universal approach. Although this particular traditional Hebrew prayer refers only to the "people Israel," our community of God's people has grown. Even in the Middle Ages, it was a principle of Jewish law that we should pray for all people facing illness, regardless of their religion or background (*Shulchan Aruch, Yoreh Deah* 335:9).

If you can pray for yourself in the midst of community, Jewish tradition deems this a very powerful prayer. "A prayer for oneself when ill is more effective than those of anyone else" (Genesis Rabbah 53:14). You may not be used to thinking of yourself this way. It may be easier for you to pray for and worry about others. But you are deserving of your own prayers. Only you know what is truly in your own heart.

What Kind of Powerful?

Even before we open our mouths to say a prayer, we have already done something very significant. By being willing to pray, we acknowledge that God is more powerful than we are. The Rabbis had a very specific idea of what "God's power" means. You might think of splitting seas, shattering mountains, or great explosions. You might envision floods or plagues of locusts and lice. Biblical tradition gives many examples of the destructive forces attributed to God. Many understand God as a King who rewards and punishes, who fixes things or chooses not to, including our bodies. Too often our first thoughts of God are as an admonishing Lord.

Contrast these notions with a description in a prayer from the siddur:

> Your power is infinite, O Exalted One, who gives life. You sustain the living with devotion, with great compassion You give life to the dead. You lift up the falling, heal the sick, free the captive, and You keep faith with those who sleep in the dust. Who is like You, O Powerful One? To whom can You be compared, Ruler who gives death, life, and salva-

tion? For You are faithful in giving life to the dead. Praised are You, Eternal One, Giver of Life to the dead.[5]

Whereas we might normally associate power with the ability to destroy, this prayer specifically talks about rejuvenation with the metaphor of "giving life to the dead." One of the Rabbis' names for God is "Giver of Life." For some, the power ascribed to "giving life to the dead" was literally true, because they believed in resurrection,[6] but for many today it means reviving the lifeless in any fashion. Many Jews now understand this prayer figuratively, implying that which revives us or gives us new meaning. God is also described as not only healing the sick but also supporting those who fall, sustaining the living with kindness, and setting free captives.

> You might choose to see God's power manifested in reviving spirits, in rejuvenating relationships, in newfound freedom, and in the sustaining power of kindness.

Not only Jews today but also Jews in ancient times had a broad understanding of what it meant to "give life." Consider, for instance, the custom in Judaism that if you have not seen a friend for over a year and then you finally see him or her, the traditional blessing you say is "Praised are You, Eternal One our God, Ruler of the universe, who gives life to the dead." The resurrection of a friendship is seen here as life-giving.

But illness might estrange us from ourselves. We might not only literally be brought back to life from physical danger but we might also discover that a new kind of life awaits us.

Faced with our mortality, we might want a fresh start and a break from old habits or behavior, a second chance. Recovering from illness can mean the beginning of a new life. Today, you might choose to see God's power manifested in reviving spirits, in rejuvenating relationships, in newfound freedom, and in the sustaining power of kindness.

The Morning, Afternoon, and Evening of Your Life

A passage from the Jerusalem Talmud defines the meaning of prayer in Judaism, and it speaks to us at all times, healthy or not:

> From where have we learned that there are three moments for prayer? Rabbi Sh'muel bar Nachmani taught that it corresponds with the three times of the day that are distinguishable to all humanity:
>
> In the morning, a person should say, "I give thanks before You, my God and God of my ancestors, that You have brought me from darkness to light."
>
> In the afternoon, a person should say, "I give thanks before You, my God and God of my ancestors, that just as You have enabled me to see the sun in the east, so have You enabled me to see it set in the west."
>
> In the evening, a person should say, "May it be Your will, Compassionate One, my God and God of my ancestors,

that just as I was in darkness and You brought me out of it to the light that You will bring me out of darkness to light again."

JERUSALEM TALMUD, *BERACHOT* 4:1, 29B

It is a Jewish tradition to pray three times a day. This passage gives one set of reasons why this is so. Rabbi Sh'muel bar Nachmani believes that there are three times during the day that all human beings have an opportunity to pray, to see a larger reality beyond themselves. He claims that this opportunity goes beyond the Jewish community. It is universal "to all humanity."

In the morning, a person gives thanks. God brings us from darkness to light. We wake up in the morning, the darkness of night has disappeared, and we are privileged to see a new day. There is a daily cycle to our lives that should not be taken for granted. Each new day is a precious gift, and we get to live and breathe, work and play, love and connect with others. It is a privilege to exist.

In the afternoon, we should also still have a feeling of gratitude. Just as we saw the sun rise, so do we also get to see it set. We are able to see tasks completed, aspirations fulfilled, and the people around us grow into new stages of life. Although there is certainly much left undone, there has also been another day of fulfillment. We can allow ourselves to feel a certain amount of contentment.

In the evening, however, when it is dark, the Talmud does not ask that we give thanks for what we have seen and done. It changes focus. At night, when we naturally are afraid of the dark, we petition God. The prayer in the dark is one where we ask for help. We pray that we make it through the darkness. Just as we have been through the night before, so too do we pray we get through a dark time and see the light again.

This cycle of prayers is clearly about more than experiencing a new day. It is also about hope during dark times of challenge. We are grateful for what each day brings us, and we petition God when it is night in our lives. There are moments when we feel cold and cannot see. We try to be hopeful during times when the darkness seems overwhelming. We remember that there have been other times of difficulty, and we have survived those moments. We can face similar moments with determination and strength.

On a different and even deeper level, this passage also teaches us about the possibilities of the entire span of a person's life. If we understand that "morning," "afternoon," and "evening" refer not to a day but to a lifetime, then we get a different picture. In the morning, we are grateful for existing, for the blessing of life. We are filled with childlike wonder. We are grateful for our growth. In the afternoon of our lifetime, we might similarly feel grateful for our accomplishments. We might give thanks for a full career, for anniversaries, or for the growth of our children whom we have seen become adults. In the evening, when we are facing our inevitable end, we might put our hope in some kind of afterlife or simply peace of mind. Just as we have left some things undone, so were there also many things that we tried to do. We might petition God for a new kind of light, an enlightenment of acceptance and peace.

One of the most well-known Jewish prayers said in the evening of our lives is the Mourner's Kaddish. This is a prayer praising God for life that is said at the conclusion of every Jewish prayer service, and it is done with great solemnity in memory of those who have died. It is composed in complicated yet rhythmic Aramaic. Many Jews have a visceral, emotional reaction to its sound. The Mourner's Kaddish is a prayer that evokes memories in the hearts of millions of Jews. It is called the Mourner's Kaddish because we say it in memory of people who have died. In Hebrew, its name literally translates to the "Orphan's Kaddish" because it is said by children in memory of their parents. Personally, I always associate this prayer with nighttime because I grew up going to Shabbat services on Friday nights, and it was the last prayer said when it was already quite dark outside.

Even though the prayer is one of mourning, it does not mention death. This is because initially the prayer had nothing to do with mourning at all. The prayer was placed (as it still is in the siddur) to be recited upon completing a rubric of prayer during a worship service or upon completing a book of sacred study in the ancient Jewish academies. When the study of a volume of Talmud or other holy volume was finished, the class would recite a version of Kaddish. Kaddish comes from the Hebrew word for holiness. The words are a doxology, an overflowing praise of the holiness of God for having finished a part of something sacred.

> If prayer is supposed to help us think about the morning, afternoon, and evening of our lives, it might be helpful to think of our lives as a book. What kind of words are we writing with our actions each day?

The symbolism of Kaddish as a statement of completion takes on a new layer of meaning during Rosh Hashanah, the Jewish New Year, and Yom Kippur, the Day of Atonement. During these days Jews think about what they have completed and what they have left undone. In the liturgy, we ask God to inscribe us "in the Book of Life." The Book of Life is a metaphor mentioned on these sacred days to make us imagine God recording our deeds in a book with all of our personalized chapters and paragraphs. At the turn of the year, we ask God to write another chapter in our spiritual books, as if each one of our lives is a volume waiting to be completed. Just as the Kaddish was once said for the completion of an actual book, so too did this prayer come to be said at the conclusion of a life, at the end of a person's book. When a person's sacred Book of Life is completed, when a life is over, we now say Kaddish.

If prayer is supposed to help us think about the morning, afternoon, and evening of our lives—especially in the face of illness—it might be helpful to think of our lives as a book. What kind of words are we writing with our actions each day, and what kind of example are we setting, especially in how to face adversity? What is the next chapter in our Book of Life?

When You Need
to Scream

My wife, Julie, once faced a serious illness. Thankfully, she is completely recovered, but we still remember that time vividly. The day before our daughter's fourth birthday, she suffered a severe pain in her belly. It became so acute that she doubled over and could not straighten up. Calling the babysitter over to spend the night, we drove through an icy winter storm to the emergency room.

The doctors figured out that something was wrong with her intestines, that they had become twisted into a knot. Although it was a very long night, they were able to give her relief. She was smiling by morning. She did, however, need surgery so that it would not happen again.

The day of the surgery arrived. Julie prayed out loud for her recovery. I held her hand and prayed with her. Whenever anyone had to stick her with a needle (she hates needles; who doesn't?), she would sing Rabbi Nachman of Breslov's song of bravery, *Kol haolam kulo, gesher tzar m'od, v'ha-ikar lo l'fached klal,* "All of the world is a very narrow bridge, but the important thing is not to be afraid." The nurses looked at us a little funny when she would sing (neither one of us can carry a tune), but honestly we were so fearful that we didn't care. Julie also took deep breaths whenever the pain would come. She says she learned that when she gave birth to our children: "I just have to breathe through it."

During the surgery, I waited with family and friends in a very small waiting room that had a television hanging from the ceiling. I watched more daytime television than I ever had before. During those long hours, I discovered a small chapel adjacent to the waiting room. The pews were so close together that I could barely fit into a seat. Nevertheless, I felt reassured that the room was there, even if it was uncomfortable. It was as if prayers, even if they were hypothetical, were somehow part of the process.

> Prayer is simply talking to God, even if it is entirely in your mind. You can even scream in your mind.

The surgery came and went, and all looked well. It was a tremendous relief to see her in the recovery room. We all let go of our breath because Julie was on her way to recovery. Soon, we were back to waiting with her at her bedside. I had prepared all sorts of things that I thought she might want: a CD player with her favorite music, a collage of photographs of our children, and an assortment of other things I knew would make her feel more comfortable.

The recovery was going so well that Julie insisted that I get out of the room and do some work. I could even travel out of town for a day. "What do I need you here for? I'm fine. Go!" I made the mistake of listening to her.

I received a call that I had to come to the hospital right away. Something inside of her was leaking, and she was running a fever. She needed another emergency operation. I drove as fast as I could to the hospital with the doctor's words still ringing in my ears: "You need to see your wife before surgery."

Did this mean that she might not make it? What was going on? How could this be? We had a four-year-old and a three-year-old. How could I have left her alone?

I made it seconds before they took her in and was able to tell her how much I loved her. She has since said that waiting for me to come was one of the most grueling ordeals of her life.

They wheeled her in for the operation, and I still could not get my mind around what was happening. Was this real? How was this happening? I returned to the waiting room with its other people and its hanging television, and I needed to scream.

What could I do? Another family was waiting for news about their loved one. Oprah was talking about the best way to cook pasta. The chapel was so cramped that I could not fit in it, and besides, I needed to be near the intercom in case they called me.

I thought of Julie singing Rabbi Nachman's song. Somehow, I recalled another teaching of his about prayer. He taught that praying is simply talking to God, even if it is entirely in your mind. You can even scream in your mind by imagining the loudness of your voice.

I began to scream silently. "Please help my wife!" I screamed with my lips shut. "Please help my wife!" Each time I screamed louder and louder until I literally felt my body shaking, vibrating with emotion. "PLEASE HELP MY WIFE!"

The other people in the room did not notice a thing. After what seemed like an endless period of time, I was called to the doctor to be told that everything was okay.

Fortunately, they were able to fix what was wrong. Yet another surgery was required, but at least she was out of danger. What was supposed to be a few days in the hospital turned into a month in the intensive care unit. It was a very long ordeal.

We are very fortunate that everything turned out positively. Julie has no complications and is completely recovered. Recovering emotionally, however, took much longer. It was a nightmare we both lived through, and when we look back at that time, we try to remember it without having to relive it.

You can scream if you need to. Rabbi Nachman teaches that sometimes just to get through the moment, you can "pour out your cry to God" (Psalm 142:3). Judaism affirms that God always hears, even when we feel lost and shut out from all that is good in the world. "Even if all gates are tightly shut, the Gate of Tears is always open" (*Zohar, Terumah* 165).[7]

Why Prayer Works Even When It Doesn't

The goal of prayer in Judaism is humility. Life is never what we expect it will be, and it is usually when our egos have been damaged and we are forced to look deeply into ourselves that we discover meaning. Even in lofty moments of celebration, we should remember to be humble. A man named Rabbi Yosi understood this:

> Rabbi Yosi the son of Rabbi Chanina taught in the name of Rabbi Eliezer ben Ya'akov: One should not stand on a high place when one prays but should rather stand in a lowly place, as it is written, "Out of the low places I called to You, Eternal God."
>
> BABYLONIAN TALMUD, *BERACHOT* 10A ON PSALM 130:1

Rabbi Yosi understood, as taught to him by his teachers, that being in high places can be unhealthy for our attitude and our spirit. The air is too thin up there. We can get caught up in our own importance and our need to rule over all aspects of our life. Too often, when we stay up in the heights of our egos too long, we are brought down to size by life's challenges.

No matter how high we are, we should never forget the basic hierarchy of religious life: God is above and we are below.

If we have a healthy attitude of humility, if we remember that we are not at the center of the universe but that we exist as part of a larger whole, if we understand a greater reality beyond ourselves, then we can stand in the lowly places with courage. If we remember that every place, in relation to God, is a lowly place, then we can remember our proper stance as human beings.

> If we have a healthy attitude of humility, if we understand a greater reality beyond ourselves, then we can stand in the lowly places with courage.

To pray, therefore, is to remember our proper place, to consciously lower ourselves if we have become too haughty. It might serve as a reminder to return to a humble stance that is not only more honest but also less stressful and healthier for our souls.

Finding the Simple Truth in Prayer

The Jewish morning liturgy contains a prayer specifically about how our bodies work and our health. It may sound primitive to our ears or too graphic for the squeamish to qualify as a prayer, for we are used to prayer being articulated in lofty language. Despite our modern sensibilities, these are the words that the Rabbis of antiquity chose to say each morning. The prayer reads as follows:

> Praised are You, the Eternal our God, Ruler of the universe, who has formed humanity with wisdom and created within a person many orifices and valves. It is revealed and known before Your throne of glory that if one of them were to open or close improperly, then it would be impossible to endure and stand before You. Praised are You, Eternal One, Healer of all flesh and Maker of miracles.

In prayer we are accustomed to words like "wisdom" and "glory," but "orifices" and "valves"? What kind of prayer is this? Perhaps a few biology teachers might find such language edifying, but what about the rest of us?

One of my colleagues in rabbinical school was Rabbi Scott Hausman-Weiss. He married a wonderful woman named Natalie, and they decided to have children. While Scott was still in school, little Abraham entered their lives. What immediately became clear was the nightmare that all parents fear: something was wrong. The growth of the sheath around Abraham's spinal cord did not develop properly. After several surgeries, these new parents had to face the shocking

> Our body is made up of miracles of openings and closings that work to the beat of an extraordinary Maker.

fact that their child was never going to walk. He was never going to kick a ball or run. The orifices and valves below Abraham's waist did not work properly, and Abraham was never going to stand. He was going to face an entirely different kind of life than his parents had envisioned.

Some time after this shocking revelation, Scott told me, "What I came to realize is that most medical problems basically boil down to something not opening or closing properly. It's about flaps in the body. Either the flap opens when it shouldn't or is closed when it shouldn't be. I have never been able to read the prayer from the morning liturgy about the human body in the same way since Abraham was born."

As Abraham grew, his family discovered new things, the kinds of things that no one understands unless they have to. Wheelchairs, for instance, come in all sizes. Soon, miniature wheelchairs entered into their lives, and when most children were learning to walk and run, Abraham was learning to push himself around.

To use the phrase "confined to a wheelchair," however, would be completely inappropriate for this child. This child is not "confined" at all. Those who have the privilege of knowing this family have inevitably seen Abraham whizzing by. He gets up to speed and makes sharp turns with the casual competence of a race-car driver. His sharp mind and contagious smile accompany what can only be called an indomitable spirit. To see this child on the move is uplifting to anyone with a feeling heart.

The prayer from the morning liturgy says that if these orifices and valves did not open and close properly, we would not be able to stand before our Maker. Indeed, Abraham is not able to stand. In another place in the Jewish tradition, however, we read of a different kind of existence before God, one that is beyond most people's understanding. In the first chapter of the book of Ezekiel, the prophet Ezekiel has a vision of God. It is a vision of exaltation and mystery. In this vision, God is seated on a chariot with wheels and angels whirling around.

Jewish mystics of later centuries felt this was one of the most important passages in the Bible. They felt it was a key to understanding God, and they studied this image of God sitting on a throne in a chariot, riding over the palaces of heaven. It was the goal of many of these Jewish mystics to reach such an intuitive understanding of how God works within their bodies and souls that they would "descend into the chariot" to directly comprehend the miracle and blessing of existence.

Although we often stand in religious services as a sign of respect, as if we are standing in front of God's throne, anyone who sees Abraham also knows that "standing before the throne of glory" is only one image among many. Some do not need to stand. Some are seated in the throne itself and ride in God's chariot.

Abraham's father reflects on his son's extraordinary talents and has come to some sense of peace, although every new transition presents unforeseen challenges. He once told me, "I realized that during the pregnancy, I had asked God for a son who would be a blessing. I hadn't asked God for a son who could walk, only that he would be a blessing. Didn't God, in fact, give us what we wanted?"

The prayer in the morning liturgy reflects a daily reality many of us might take for granted. Anyone who has been through what Abraham's family has experienced cannot take words such as "orifices" and "valves" as mundane. They become holy words full of meaning. Similarly, anyone who has ever had any kind of medical complication might realize that our body is made up of miracles of openings and closings that work to the beat of an extraordinary Maker. They remind us of a reality that transcends our everyday experience and reaches up to the highest realms of the Divine.

God Is Right Here
and Right Now

A difficult but central belief for a Jewish theology of healing for today is a deep understanding of God being present in our lives. Many people might say that this is well and good for "believers," but what about the rest of us? Belief, however, does not have to be limited to faith in a Big Man Upstairs Who Controls Everything. God's presence instead can be thought of as an abiding, loving strength within people and all creation. In fact, the deepest things most of us believe in, such as truth, love, and compassion, are intangible but real parts of ourselves. Trying to live without confidence in a spiritual reality is like trying to live in a big black hole of despair. An unexpected touch of kindness from another can renew our faith that there is an inescapable power of goodness in the world.

This belief is rooted in the Hebrew Bible in the book of Psalms. Many people turn to the psalms for solace and for their acknowledgment of suffering, and much has been written about using the psalms in prayer. (See recommended reading for books on reading the psalms.) The psalms have also served as inspiration for all subsequent Jewish poetry. Perhaps the reason the psalms speak to so many people is because in the psalms God is understood to be present and available to people everywhere and at all times:

> How can I escape from Your spirit?
> How can I flee from Your face?
> If I go up to heaven, there You are;
> if I go down to the pit, You are here.
> If I lift up on the wings of dawn,
> lay down on the far edge of the sea,
> also there Your hand will guide me,
> Your right hand will grasp me tight.
> If I say, "But darkness will hide me,
> night will be my light,"
> darkness is not too dark for You;
> night is as bright as day;
> as is the darkness, so is the light.
>
> *Psalm* 139:7–12

It is precisely in the darkest moments that the Psalmist asks us to turn to God who is everywhere: "Out of the depths I call to You, Eternal One! Sovereign, listen to my voice!" (Psalm 130:1–2). Even in a place where we feel completely abandoned and alone or whenever we try to run away and not face the challenges before us, our biblical ancestors had faith that God was there with us. The prophet Jeremiah echoed this theme when he declared, "'Am I a God who is only nearby,' says the Eternal, 'and not [also] God from far away? If

> God is with both the one in need of healing who suffers and the one who tries to heal.

someone hides in a hiding place, can I not see him?' says the
Eternal. 'For do I not fill heaven and earth?'" (Jeremiah
23:23–24).

Solomon ibn Gabirol, a Hebrew poet from Spain, articulated the idea of God's omnipresence and the futility of running away from God with this memorable line: "I flee from
You to You."[8] Even as we hustle from chore to chore, from
office to home and home to office, from house to emergency
room, we are not abandoned by God. God is everywhere. God
is with the person who is sick in the room right here and now,
and God is also with those who care for that person as they
heed God's commandments by providing medical care, visiting,
calling, or simply sending a note. God is with both the one
in need of healing who suffers and the one who tries to heal.
The God-like in us reaches out to the God-like in another.
Dimensions of the Divine reach toward each other.

The Sages even took the idea of God's omnipresence another
radical step, surpassing the idea of God being the soul of the
universe. In their thinking, it is a mistake to think of God as a
person or a power floating around the universe. For them, God
is not only within the world, but God also transcends it. The
universe does not contain God. Instead, God contains the universe. The Rabbis articulated this belief in this way: "The Holy
One of Blessing is the dwelling place of the world; it is not the
world that is the dwelling place of God" (Genesis Rabbah
68:9). God is both near and far.[9] God is close by in the commandments we follow and in the prayers we say, and yet God
is also incomprehensibly above and beyond our understanding.
One prayer book puts it this way, "You are as close to us as
breathing, yet You are farther than the farthermost star."[10]

If we believe that God can be found within and through
people, if we believe that there is no place devoid of God's pres-

ence and love, and if we believe that there is no place where we may not pray and access the Divine, then we have to believe that God is present with us right here and right now. In every home, in every bedroom, in every building, and in every hospital room or hospice care facility, God is there. Even as you, the reader, hold this book, God is in the room with you right now.

The End of
the Matter
Gratitude

Laura had extremely long and beautiful hair. I became acquainted with her at Jewish prayer services for Shabbat on Friday nights at a nearby university. I did not know her very well, but she always seemed friendly. It was also very hard to miss her hair, which went down to her waist. Different people often spoke each week at these services, giving their interpretation of the week's Torah portion or simply giving an inspired message for all to hear. One Friday evening, she got up in front of the group to talk about what a certain passage from the Torah meant to her. She took this moment as an opportunity to speak personally. Much to everyone's shock, she told us that she was actually losing her hair because, as her close friends already knew, she was fighting cancer and taking a tremendous amount of medicine, the side effects of which seemed as bad as the illness itself. The fact that such a young person was in danger of losing her life shook us all to the core.

Despite how terrified we were on her behalf, Laura spoke with calm and poise. She had an air of peace about her. That week's Torah portion included the section on building God's sanctuary in the wilderness. Laura took this moment as an opportunity not only to grapple with her religion but also to thank those who helped her as she faced illness. Her example of *shalom* taught all of us how God can be manifest in the world, just as those who helped her compelled us to do the same for our own loved ones.

Some of her remarks from that evening, which she shared with me, went as follows. It is an honor to share them here:

"The Eternal One spoke to Moses: Speak to the people Israel and accept gifts for Me. From any person whose heart is so moved you shall accept gifts for Me.... Make Me a sanctuary, and I will dwell with them...." (Exodus 25:1–2, 25:8).

Where is God Monday, Wednesday, and Friday mornings when I have to lie down on the radiation table for thirty minutes only to come home and vomit? The doctor asks me the same questions each time I come in:

Do you feel cotton mouth? Yes. Trouble swallowing? Yes. Swollen glands? Yes. Feverish? Yes. Fatigue? Yes. Sweats? Yes. Loss of appetite? Yes. Vomiting? Yes.

The snowball effect of these treatments partnered with the plaguish thought that I am fighting for my life against a disease that is somehow eating away at my respiratory system lends me no easy time for me to evaluate my faith in God or play a guessing game as to God's whereabouts when I need God the most....

"The Eternal One spoke to Moses: Speak to the people Israel and accept gifts for Me. From any person whose heart is so moved you shall accept gifts for Me."

Thursday afternoon, I come home and take my daily dose of afternoon medications with three jars of baby food given to me by a friend who thought that baby food would go down and come up easier than "real" food. After a television show, I am visited by another friend who "just wants to keep me company" and has the unfortunate task of holding my head and stomach while I get sick. I go to work to answer phones, and my boss is nice enough to pay me for basically sitting and watching people go by, and three of the nicest people there in the college dormitory sit and keep me company. People call intermittently just to see how I'm doing.

> From any person whose heart is so moved you shall accept gifts for Me.... Make Me a sanctuary, and I will dwell with them....
>
> EXODUS 25:1–2, 25:8

"From any person whose heart is so moved you shall accept gifts for Me."

The gifts in the Torah made the dwelling place for God possible. The small kindnesses that people have given me make me feel better than the pain medication. And I start to cry. I am not a rabbi or a Torah scholar. I am just scared. But I begin to realize that within the *mitzvah* of all these gifts, my friends have built a place for me a little less frightening where, while I live, these gifts will carry me (not the other way around) to a place of strength and love and where, if I pass on, I will be remembered. And in the tiny *mitzvah*, a quick call, a jar of baby food, an honest embrace: this is where God is. The first words that I have to say are "Thank you."

Wrestling in Prayer

Ⲟne last meeting with our angel.

The Torah tells a story about the patriarch Jacob who wrestled with a "man" in the middle of the night. They wrestled until dawn when the "man," in a desperate attempt to overcome Jacob, wrenched his hip out of joint. Jacob still hung on to his opponent. Jacob realized that his wrestling partner came from God and demanded that he bless him. For his perseverance, Jacob's name was changed to "Israel," meaning that he "struggled with God and human beings and prevailed" (Genesis 32:29).

A Rabbinic retelling of this story adds some details. The name of the angel who wrestled with Jacob was Michael. God was displeased with Michael that he had wounded Jacob so severely. In response, the angel Raphael was sent to heal Jacob (*Midrash Avkir*).[11]

Judaism asks us to wrestle with God. The Jewish people are the people Israel, literally, "those who wrestle with God and humanity." In other words, we struggle with God and human life in all of its facets and limitations. This story acknowledges that both the wounding and the healing are inseparable parts of the process. The same Source that creates our bodies' function and pleasure also makes our bodies' dysfunction and pain. And the same origin for life's struggles and angst is also the Source of our healing and blessings.

Religion can be used as a tool for absolute faith, but this is a lesser form of faith. Many crave clarity and want life to be unambiguous, but the world resists such certainty. Despite all the creeds we may memorize, life takes twists we cannot predict and confronts us with questions we cannot answer.

> The same origin for life's struggles and angst is also the Source of our healing and blessings.

Absolute faith is unrealistic. It asks us to close our eyes to too many hardships, to believe in heavenly rewards we do not experience and to deny pain that confronts us every day. This form of religion might deepen our pain rather than alleviate it.

Rather, religion is better used as a way of coping than as a source of certainty. Life and death are mysteries. We can turn to prayer to talk out our sorrows and share our joys. We can appreciate the spirituality of our relationships to help us get through the day. We struggle and we wrestle, we question and we strive, and at the end of the day, all of the pain and beauty of the world are God's. We surrender knowing little more than we did as children.

One angel comes with struggle one day, and another comes with healing the next. The sun rises and sets on the world's terrible beauty and will do so long after we are gone. We are not asked to have all the answers. We are asked to hang on and to draw blessings whenever we can.

APPENDIX I
Rabbi Nachman's Silent Scream

Rabbi Nachman of Breslov's teachings about prayer, especially in a time of crisis, have been very helpful to me personally. The following two passages are excerpted from *Sichot HaRan*, "Talks with Rabbi Nachman," translated by Rabbi Aryeh Kaplan. They can be found in *Outpouring of the Soul* (Jerusalem: Breslov Research Institute, 1980), 35, 47–48, as well as *Rabbi Nachman's Wisdom* by Rabbi Nathan of Nemirov (Brooklyn: Breslov Research Institute, 1973), 112, 118–119.

> It is very good to pour out one's thoughts before God (Psalm 142:3), like a child pleading before its parent (*Mishnah Ta'anit* 3:8).
>
> God calls us His children, as it is written, "You are children to God your Lord" (Deuteronomy 14:1). Therefore, it is good to express one's thoughts and troubles to God, as a child complains to his father and pesters him.
>
> SICHOT HARAN 7

> You can shout loudly in a "small still voice" (1 Kings 19:12). With this soundless "small still voice," you can scream without anyone else hearing you.

Anyone can do this. Just imagine the sound of such a scream in your mind. Depict the shout in your imagination exactly as it would sound. Keep doing this until you are literally screaming with the soundless "small still voice."

When you depict this scream in your mind, the sound is actually ringing inside your brain. You can stand in a crowded room screaming in this manner, and no one will hear you.

Sometimes when you do this, some sound may escape your lips. The voice reverberating in your nerves may activate your vocal organs. They might then produce some sound, but it will be very faint.

It is much easier to shout this way without words. If you wish to express words, it is much more difficult to hold the voice in your mind, and not let any sound escape. Without words it is much easier.

SICHOT HARAN 16

Laws on Visiting the Sick

from the *Shulchan Aruch* of Rabbi Joseph Karo
and Rabbi Moses Isserles, *Yoreh Deah* 335

Jewish law is a rich resource for guidelines on what we ought to do and how we ought to do it. Jewish law embodies ethics and practical advice. We must also remember that different codes of Jewish law were written in different contexts and are thus products of their time. Just as they offer us guidance, they also refer to a world with a certain level of technology as well as the prejudices and assumptions of their century. We should therefore approach Jewish law codes critically, looking to glean wisdom for our time from their words in an effort to respond to the question "What does God want me to do?"

Rabbi Joseph Karo (1488–1575) was a famous legal scholar who wrote a Jewish code of law called the *Shulchan Aruch*. Born in either Spain or Portugal, he eventually moved to the Land of Israel. The *Shulchan Aruch* is a legal digest summarizing Jewish law for Karo's day, reflecting his time's attitudes and insights as well as centuries of meditations on the subject of healing. The name *Shulchan Aruch* means "Set Table," as if Karo laid out all of relevant Jewish law like a table set for a meal. Because he was a Sephardi, a Jew from a Mediterranean background, the *Shulchan Aruch* failed to take into account Ashkenazic, or Central and Eastern European, practice. For this reason, Rabbi Moses Isserles (1525–1572) of Poland added annotations to the *Shulchan Aruch*, pointing out Ashkenazic custom. His additions were called *Ha-Mappah,* meaning "The Tablecloth," as a fitting addition to a set table. Taken together, many Jewish communities still hold this combined effort as authoritative Jewish law today, for it summarizes legal thought in Judaism, including previous law codes, up until the sixteenth century. The term *Shulchan Aruch* now assumes that the glosses of Isserles are included.

Reading this law code today, we must read respectfully but selectively. We stand amazed by the rabbis' sensitivity and insight; we also find the inequality of women disturbing and the medical knowledge of the time lacking. In appendix 3, we might discover some guidelines for today that will address our contemporary needs and perspectives. What follows here is an original translation of the chapter "Laws on Visiting the Sick." Because this is a collection of earlier sources and too numerous to list with each phrase, all citations are listed in the endnotes.

1. Karo: It is a divine commandment to visit the sick.[1] Relatives and friends should come immediately, and more distant acquaintances after three days. If the sick person's illness worsens suddenly [so that he might die], anyone can come immediately.[2]

2. Karo: Even a person of great social status goes to visit a person of minor social status, and even several times a day if the person is of his affinity.[3] Anyone who comes frequently is praiseworthy so long as this is not a bother to the sick person.[4]

    Isserles: There are some who say that even someone who hates [the ill person] may come and visit, but it does not appear this way to me but rather he should not come and visit, nor comfort a mourner whom he hates, so that he does not think he rejoices at his misfortune, for this can only bring him grief. Thus it appears to me.[5]

3. Karo: When one visits the sick, one does not sit on the bed, on a chair, or on a bench [so that the visitor is above the sick person looking down], but rather one enrobes oneself and sits before him [down on the floor with him], for the Divine Presence is above the sick person's head.[6]

   Isserles: This only applies when the sick person lies on the ground, so that [if one sat in a chair] one would be higher than him, but if he is lying in bed, it is permissible to sit on a chair or bench [and thus they would be on the same level].[7]

4. Karo: One does not visit a sick person during the first three hours of the day because during the morning is when a person's illness is easiest, and one might not think to pray for compassion on his behalf [thinking the sick person does not need the prayer]. [One also does not visit] during the last three hours of the day because that is when a person's illness is hardest, and one might despair and not pray for compassion on his behalf [thinking that the person is a lost cause].[8]

   Isserles: Anyone who visits [the sick] and does not pray for him has not fulfilled his sacred obligation.[9]

5. Karo: When one prays for compassion [on behalf of someone who is ill], if one prays in his presence, one may pray in any language that one wants. But if one is not praying in his presence [and is praying in the synagogue], one may only pray in Hebrew [as part of the regular Hebrew prayer service].[10]

6. Karo: One should include [a sick person] with all others who are ill among the people Israel [when one prays] and say, "May God have compassion upon you among all others who are ill among the people Israel." On Shabbat one says, "On Shabbat we do not cry out; healing will come soon."[11]

7. Karo: People should tell [the sick person] to think of his affairs, if he has loaned or deposited anything with others, or if others have loaned or deposited anything with him.

[And one should tell him] not to fear because of this from death [that is, putting one's affairs in order does not invite death].[12]

8. Karo: People should not visit anyone with intestinal illness, eye problems, or headaches. So also anyone whose sickness is overwhelming [literally, "the world is heavy upon them"] and speech is hard for him should not be visited in person,[13] but rather people should come into an outer chamber of the house and ask and inquire of him whether they need to help clean or rinse anything, or similar things, and they should listen to his pain and pray for compassion on his behalf.[14]

9. Karo: People should visit the sick of gentiles for the sake of peace.[15]

10. Karo: For intestinal illnesses, a man may not wait upon a woman, but a woman may wait upon a man.[16]

   Isserles: There are those who say that if someone has a person who is ill in his house, he should go to the sage of the city for him to pray on his behalf.[17] So also it is a custom to bless the sick in the synagogue and also to give the sick a new name, for a change in the name rips up the decree of judgment.[18] Comforting mourners takes precedence over visiting the sick.[19]

Appendix III

Some Guidelines for Visiting the Sick in Today's World, Based on Jewish Tradition

- **Call, knock, and ask:** If the person is not well known to you, call first and make sure it is okay to visit. When you show up at the hospital room, knock first and ask whether it is okay to come in now or whether the person would prefer you to come back later. Simply asking is the best way to avoid putting the sick person in an embarrassing or stressful situation, and more often than not, the person in the hospital will be grateful that you are there. "Anyone who comes frequently is praiseworthy so long as this is not a bother to the sick person" (*Shulchan Aruch, Yoreh Deah* 335:2).

- **Try to relax:** Remember, showing up is more important than knowing what to say, for "it is a divine commandment to visit the sick" (*Shulchan Aruch, Yoreh Deah* 335:1). Try to relax yourself as much as possible before entering the room, and if you are anxious, remember that God is in the room with you as a source of comfort, strength, and life.

- **Bring something and take something away:** Bring some kind of small gift. Some congregations have children in the religious school make art projects for delivery to hospitals. Flowers are sometimes okay but often too fragrant. (Incidentally, this also means avoiding wearing perfume or cologne.) Remember, you may give a gift, but you also take away a fraction of the other's suffering, even if you cannot see it.

- **Sit down:** Sit down so that you are at eye level with the person. Being at the same level invites a sense of equality and empathy, rather than looming over a person, hence the saying, "the Divine Presence is above the sick person's head" (*Shulchan Aruch, Yoreh Deah* 335:3). This also means respecting another's personal space, so always ask before touching a bed rail or a wheelchair or sitting on the bed if there is not a chair.

- **Be very careful before visiting someone with whom you have a personal conflict:** Make sure that you call first. Visiting, calling, or sending a gift to someone who is ill can be a catalyst for healing a relationship as well as someone's body and spirit. Someone who is ill may not have the energy to also deal with personal issues, however, so simply calling or sending a gift usually suffices.

- **Listen more than you speak:** Pay close attention to what the person is saying and the expression on the person's face. Acknowledge what the person is saying by repeating back words or phrases that the person uses, so that the person feels heard, as it says, "listen to his [or her] pain" (*Shulchan Aruch, Yoreh Deah* 335:8).

- **Pray:** Pray for the person who is ill, Jewish or not Jewish, young or old, male or female, rich or poor, in any language, both inside and outside the hospital. You can do this directly to a person by simply saying, "I pray you have a *r'fuah sh'leimah*, a complete healing of body and spirit." Include the people who you know are ill in prayers for healing at your place of worship, and send them a card letting them know that you prayed for them during prayer services. This will help them feel more connected with their community.

Notes

Part One—Reaching Inward: Coping When You Are Ill

1. Tony Kushner, *Angels in America* (New York: Theatre Communications Group, 1995), part 1, "Millennium Approaches," act 2, scene 1.

2. I use the English words "soul" and "spirit" interchangeably, although there are many Jewish sources that have more specific meanings attached to particular Hebrew terms, specifically *nefesh* and *neshamah*, usually translated as "soul" and "spirit," respectively. Rabbi Moses ben Maimon, Maimonides or Rambam (1135–1204), for instance, distinguishes between an "animal soul" and an "intellectual spirit" in his treatise on the soul, *Shemonah Perakim*.

3. Quoted in Avraham Yaakov Finkel, *In My Flesh I See God: A Treasury of Rabbinic Insights about the Human Anatomy* (Northvale, NJ: Jason Aronson, 1995), 303.

4. Rabbi Nachman of Breslov, *Advice* (Jerusalem: Breslov Research Institute, 1983), 253.

5. Henri J. Nouwen, *Creative Ministry: Beyond Professionalism in Teaching, Preaching, Counseling, Organizing, and Celebrating* (Garden City, NY: Doubleday & Company, 1971), xiv–xv.

6. Translation from David Polish, *Rabbi's Manual* (New York: Central Conference of American Rabbis, 1988), 108–9.

7. In Lawrence Hoffman, ed., *My People's Prayer Book: Traditional Prayers, Modern Commentaries,* vol. 1, *The* Sh'ma *and Its Blessings* (Woodstock, VT: Jewish Lights, 1997), 109.

8. Consider the words of Maimonides about health being a product of hygiene: "As long as a person takes active exercise, works hard, does not overeat and keeps his bowels open, he will be free from disease and increase in vigor, even though the food he eats is coarse." *Mishneh Torah,* Laws of Attributes 4, as cited in Jacob Minkin, *The World of Moses Maimonides* (New York: Thomas Yoseloff, 1957), 384.

9. See also Babylonian Talmud, *Sanhedrin* 73a; Babylonian Talmud, *Bava Kamma* 81b; and Deuteronomy 22:2, where restoring one's lost property is understood to include the health of one's body. For two summaries of these laws, see Elliot Dorff, *Matters of Life and Death* (Philadelphia: Jewish Publication Society, 2003), 26–29; or Mark Washofsky, *Jewish Living* (New York: UAHC Press, 2001), 220–24.

10. There is a story of a man who was ill, and the sages Rabbi Akiba and Rabbi Ishmael prescribed a cure. When they were challenged on their action and accused of tampering with God's will, they responded that just as a farmer uses a sickle to glean a vineyard, so too is medicine a legitimate tool given to us by God. *Otzar Midrashim* 580, *Midrash Temurah* 2 (New York, 1915).

11. As taught to me by Rabbi M. Bruce Lustig.

12. This was taught by Rabbi Sheldon Zimmerman at Hebrew Union College–Jewish Institute of Religion in Cincinnati, 1999.

13. Quoted in Finkel, *In My Flesh*, 7.

Part Two—Reaching Outward: Finding Strength in Caregiving

1. Rabbi Nachman of Breslov, *The Empty Chair: Finding Hope and Joy— Timeless Wisdom from a Hasidic Master, Rebbe Nachman of Breslov*, adapted by Moshe Mykoff (Woodstock, VT: Jewish Lights, 1996), 9, 20.

2. Sylvia Boorstein, *Don't Just Do Something, Sit There: A Mindfulness Retreat with Sylvia Boorstein* (San Francisco: HarperCollins, 1996).

3. "A Healing Broth," in *Hasidic Tales: Annotated & Explained*, trans. and ann. Rami Shapiro (Woodstock, VT: SkyLight Paths, 2004), 71.

4. Some believe that there is a mistake in the text, and the correct name is Rabbi Abba. Rather than emend the text, I have left it as it appears in the Talmud.

5. There is an alternative version of this lesson in Leviticus Rabbah 34:1. There, Rabbi Huna states that sixty people can come and cure a person all at once, but only if they "love him like themselves" (Leviticus 19:18).

6. See Kerry M. Olitzky and Stuart A. Copans, *Twelve Jewish Steps to Recovery: A Personal Guide to Turning from Alcoholism and Other Addictions—Drugs, Food, Gambling, Sex ...* 2nd ed. (Woodstock, VT: Jewish Lights, 2009), xxxi.

Part Three—Gathering Around: Dealing with Family

1. For an excellent exploration of these themes, see Norman Cohen, *Self, Struggle, and Change: Family Conflict Stories in Genesis and Their Healing Insights for Our Lives* (Woodstock, VT: Jewish Lights, 1996).

2. This description of a healthy family reflects the materials of Life Innovations, Inc., based out of Minneapolis, MN, developed by Dr. David H. Olson, Dr. David G. Fournier, and Dr. Joan M. Druckman. In addition to Rabbi Edwin H. Friedman (see note 3, below), see also Lynn Hoffman, *Foundations of Family Therapy* (New York: Basic Books, 1981), and Michael E. Kerr and Murray Bowen, *Family Evaluation* (New York: W. W. Norton, 1988), of the Family Center of Georgetown University Hospital. I am personally indebted to my teacher Rabbi Julie Schwartz for being my guide through this material.

3. Edwin H. Friedman, *Generation to Generation* (New York: Guilford Press, 1985), 19–20.

Part Four—Reaching Upward: Searching for God

1. The classic exposition of wish fulfillment and dreams is in Sigmund Freud, *The Interpretation of Dreams* (New York: Avon Books, 1965), 588–611.

2. Moses Maimonides, *Guide of the Perplexed* (Chicago: University of Chicago, 1963), 139.

3. See www.abcnews.go.com, "Can Prayer Heal?" August 13, 2001.

4. For a review of some of the most recent and popular studies, see Irwin Tessman and Jack Tessman, "Efficacy of Prayer: A Critical Examination of Claims," *Skeptical Inquirer*, March/April 2000.

5. This is the second prayer of the *Amidah*, or "Standing Prayer." There are many versions currently published. The traditional Hebrew refers to God's power to give life exclusively in reference to resurrecting the dead, whereas other prayer books have changed the Hebrew to simply give life to every soul. In my translation, I have tried to combine both approaches.

6. Belief in resurrection for the righteous after the time of the Messiah was a central tenet of classic Rabbinic theology. See Ephraim E. Urbach, *The Sages: The World and Wisdom of the Rabbis of the Talmud* (Cambridge: Harvard University Press, 1979), 653.

7. Quoted in Finkel, *In My Flesh,* 122.

8. Solomon ibn Gabirol, "The Royal Crown," in *The Selected Religious Poems of Solomon ibn Gabirol,* ed. Israel Zangwill (Philadelphia: Jewish Publication Society of America, 1923), 118. The translation of the Hebrew is mine.

9. This statement is in keeping with Rabbi Leo Baeck. See "Mystery and Commandment," in *Judaism and Christianity* (Philadelphia: Jewish Publication Society of America, 1958).

10. Chaim Stern, *Gates of Prayer for Shabbat and Weekdays: A Gender Sensitive Prayerbook* (New York: Central Conference of American Rabbis, 1994), 87.

11. As cited in Hayim Nahman Bialik and Yehoshua Hanah Ravnitzky, eds., *The Book of Legends/Sefer Ha-Aggadah: Legends from the Talmud and Midrash* (New York: Schocken Books, 1992), 49.

Appendix II: Laws on Visiting the Sick

1. Babylonian Talmud, *Sotah* 14a; and *Tanchuma, Vayera* 1. According to the Sages, it is not only a divine commandment from the Torah to visit the sick, but it is also an instance of imitating God, for it is God who performs this duty in Rabbinic legend. God appears to Abraham after Abraham's circumcision as an act of visiting the sick, setting an example for human beings to follow.

2. Maimonides in the *Mishneh Torah*, Laws for a Mourner 14:5.

3. Babylonian Talmud, *Nedarim* 39b. The expression "of his affinity" could mean that the visitor is of the same age and therefore a peer of the sick person. This is according to Rabbi Solomon ben Isaac, Rashi (1040–1105). According to Rabbi Nissim ben Reuben of Gerona, the Ran (1290–1375), however, it means that the person is of the same astrological sign and therefore of the same temperament. In the Talmud, it appears that it is desirable to have someone "of his affinity" visit in that this is required to ease his pain; the translation might also be understood as "even if he is of his affinity," perhaps suggesting that we might hesitate to visit a peer who is so ill because it brings up our own fears and sense of mortality.

4. Rabbi Moses Maimonides, *Mishneh Torah*, Laws for a Mourner 14:4. In the Babylonian Talmud, *Nedarim* 39b, one sage teaches that we may visit even a hundred times in a day, and each person takes away a fraction of the sick person's pain.

5. Rabbi Jacob ben Moses Moellin, the Maharil (1360–1427), in Responsum 197, claims that one who hates another may still visit him when the object of his hatred becomes sick. Rabbi Elijah ben Solomon Zalman, the Vilna Gaon, suggests Rabbi Moses Isserles' objection to this is founded on Babylonian Talmud, *Sanhedrin* 19a, where a High Priest in mourning is not comforted by the anointed High Priest who has passed from office, for the anointed High Priest who has passed from office is there to take his place if something were to happen to him. Because the anointed High Priest who has passed from office is the High Priest's potential replacement, there could be some enmity between them.

6. Babylonian Talmud, *Nedarim* 40a.

7. This is attributed to Rabbi Nissim.

8. Babylonian Talmud, *Nedarim* 40a.

9. This is attributed to Rabbi Moses ben Nachman, Nachmanides or Ramban (1195–1270).

10. Babylonian Talmud, *Shabbat* 12a–b.

11. Babylonian Talmud, *Shabbat* 12a–b. On the Sabbath, we are supposed to refrain from prayers of petition.

12. Rabbi Jacob ben Asher, the Tur (1275–1343), *Arba'ah Turim, Yoreh Deah* 335.

13. Babylonian Talmud, *Nedarim* 41a.

14. The phraseology is again borrowed from Rabbi Jacob ben Asher, *Arba'ah Turim, Yoreh Deah* 335. The chores listed are reminiscent of the actions of Rabbi Akiba on behalf of one of his sick students in Babylonian Talmud, *Nedarim* 39b–40a, where it states that Rabbi Akiba swept the room and sprinkled water to keep the dust down, and this helped revive the ill student. As a result, Rabbi Akiba taught that one who does not visit the sick is like one who sheds blood.

15. Babylonian Talmud, *Gittin* 61a.

16. Rabbi David Halevi, the Taz (1586–1667), claims that intestinal illness can lead to obscenity and a man can take advantage of a woman in such a compromised state. He further claims that the reverse situation of a woman taking care of a man is not a worry because the woman's evil impulse is not as strong as a man's, so she will not do anything obscene to him. Also, or so the argument goes, he does not have the strength or will to derive any pleasure from her care. Rabbi Shabbatai Hacohen, the Shach (1621–1662), similarly claims that a man may not take care of a woman with intestinal illness because a man can take advantage of a woman in this state, but a woman physically cannot take advantage of a man. He bases his reasoning on the words of Rabbi Joseph Karo's commentary to *Arba'ah Turim, Beit Yosef*. Today, sadly, we know that both men and women can take advantage of each other sexually.

17. Babylonian Talmud, *Bava Batra* 116a.

18. Babylonian Talmud, *Rosh Hashanah* 16b.

19. The judgment that comforting mourners takes precedence over visiting the sick is based on Rabbi Moses Maimonides, *Mishneh Torah*, Laws for a Mourner 14:7, who claims that comforting mourners benefits the living and the dead, while visiting the sick benefits only the living.

Recommended Reading

If You Are Ill or Facing Another Kind of Infirmity

Haberman, Joshua. *Healing Psalms: The Dialogues with God That Help You Cope with Life.* Hoboken, NJ: John Wiley & Sons, 2003.

Kurtz, Ernest, and Katherine Ketcham. *The Spirituality of Imperfection: Storytelling and the Search for Meaning.* New York: Bantam Books, 1993.

Nachman of Breslov. *Advice.* Jerusalem: Breslov Research Institute, 1983.

———. *The Empty Chair: Finding Hope and Joy—Timeless Wisdom from a Hasidic Master, Rebbe Nachman of Breslov.* Adapted by Moshe Mykoff and the Breslov Research Institute. Woodstock, VT: Jewish Lights, 1996.

———. *The Gentle Weapon: Prayers for Everyday and Not-So-Everyday Moments.* Adapted by Moshe Mykoff and S. C. Mizrahi, together with the Breslov Research Institute. Woodstock, VT: Jewish Lights, 1999.

———. *Outpouring of the Soul.* Jerusalem: Breslov Research Institute, 1980.

Olitzky, Kerry M. *Jewish Paths toward Healing and Wholeness: A Personal Guide to Dealing with Suffering.* Woodstock, VT: Jewish Lights, 2000.

Spitz, Elie Kaplan, with Erica Shapiro Taylor. *Healing from Despair: Choosing Wholeness in a Broken World.* Woodstock, VT: Jewish Lights, 2008.

Weintraub, Simkha Y. *Healing of Soul, Healing of Body: Spiritual Leaders Unfold the Strength and Solace in Psalms.* Woodstock, VT: Jewish Lights, 1994.

If You Are a Caregiver, Clergy, or a Medical Professional

Cutter, William, ed. *Healing and the Jewish Imagination: Spiritual and Practical Perspectives on Judaism and Health.* Woodstock, VT: Jewish Lights, 2007.

Friedman, Dayle A., ed. *Jewish Pastoral Care: A Practical Handbook from Traditional and Contemporary Sources.* 2nd ed. Woodstock, VT: Jewish Lights, 2010.

Ozarowski, Joseph S. *To Walk in God's Ways: Jewish Pastoral Perspectives on Illness and Bereavement.* Lanham, MD: Rowman and Littlefield, 2004.

Richards, Marty. *Caresharing: A Reciprocal Approach to Caregiving and Care Receiving in the Complexities of Aging, Illness or Disability.* Woodstock, VT: SkyLight Paths, 2010.

Grief/Healing

Facing Illness, Finding God: How Judaism Can Help You and Caregivers Cope When Body or Spirit Fails   *By Rabbi Joseph B. Meszler*
Helps you deal with the difficulties of disease when you are questioning where God is when we get sick.   6 x 9, 208 pp, Quality PB, 978-1-58023-423-8 **$16.99**

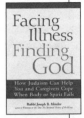

Midrash and Medicine: Healing Body and Soul in the Jewish Interpretive Tradition   *Edited by Rabbi William Cutter, PhD*   Explores how Midrash can help you see beyond the physical aspects of healing to tune in to your spiritual source.
6 x 9, 240 pp (est), HC, 978-1-58023-428-3 **$24.99**

Healing and the Jewish Imagination: Spiritual and Practical Perspectives on Judaism and Health   *Edited by Rabbi William Cutter, PhD*
6 x 9, 240 pp, Quality PB, 978-1-58023-373-6 **$19.99**; HC, 978-1-58023-314-9 **$24.99**

Grief in Our Seasons: A Mourner's Kaddish Companion   *By Rabbi Kerry M. Olitzky*
4½ x 6½, 448 pp, Quality PB, 978-1-879045-55-2 **$15.95**

Healing of Soul, Healing of Body: Spiritual Leaders Unfold the Strength & Solace in Psalms   *Edited by Rabbi Simkha Y. Weintraub, CSW*
6 x 9, 128 pp, 2-color illus. text, Quality PB, 978-1-879045-31-6 **$16.99**

Mourning & Mitzvah, 2nd Edition: A Guided Journal for Walking the Mourner's Path through Grief to Healing   *By Anne Brener, LCSW*   7½ x 9, 304 pp, Quality PB, 978-1-58023-113-8 **$19.99**

Tears of Sorrow, Seeds of Hope, 2nd Edition: A Jewish Spiritual Companion for Infertility and Pregnancy Loss   *By Rabbi Nina Beth Cardin*
6 x 9, 208 pp, Quality PB, 978-1-58023-233-3 **$18.99**

A Time to Mourn, a Time to Comfort, 2nd Edition: A Guide to Jewish Bereavement
By Dr. Ron Wolfson; Preface by Rabbi David J. Wolpe   7 x 9, 384 pp, Quality PB, 978-1-58023-253-1 **$19.99**

When a Grandparent Dies: A Kid's Own Remembering Workbook for Dealing with Shiva and the Year Beyond   *By Nechama Liss-Levinson, PhD*
8 x 10, 48 pp, 2-color text, HC, 978-1-879045-44-6 **$15.95**   *For ages 7–13*

Bible Study/Midrash

The Modern Men's Torah Commentary: New Insights from Jewish Men on the 54 Weekly Torah Portions   *Edited by Rabbi Jeffrey K. Salkin*   A major contribution to modern biblical commentary. Addresses the most important concerns of modern men by opening them up to the life of Torah.   6 x 9, 368 pp, HC, 978-1-58023-395-8 **$24.99**

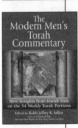

The Genesis of Leadership: What the Bible Teaches Us about Vision, Values and Leading Change   *By Rabbi Nathan Laufer; Foreword by Senator Joseph I. Lieberman*
Unlike other books on leadership, this one is rooted in the stories of the Bible.
6 x 9, 288 pp, Quality PB, 978-1-58023-352-1 **$18.99**

Hineini in Our Lives: Learning How to Respond to Others through 14 Biblical Texts and Personal Stories   *By Rabbi Norman J. Cohen, PhD*   6 x 9, 240 pp, Quality PB, 978-1-58023-274-6 **$16.99**

Moses and the Journey to Leadership: Timeless Lessons of Effective Management from the Bible and Today's Leaders   *By Rabbi Norman J. Cohen, PhD*
6 x 9, 240 pp, Quality PB, 978-1-58023-351-4 **$18.99**; HC, 978-1-58023-227-2 **$21.99**

Self, Struggle & Change: Family Conflict Stories in Genesis and Their Healing Insights for Our Lives   *By Rabbi Norman J. Cohen, PhD*   6 x 9, 224 pp, Quality PB, 978-1-879045-66-8 **$18.99**

The Triumph of Eve & Other Subversive Bible Tales   *By Matt Biers-Ariel*   5½ x 8½, 192 pp
Quality PB, 978-1-59473-176-1 **$14.99**   *(A book from SkyLight Paths, Jewish Lights' sister imprint)*

The Wisdom of Judaism: An Introduction to the Values of the Talmud
By Rabbi Dov Peretz Elkins   Explores the essence of Judaism through reflections on the words of the rabbinic sages.   6 x 9, 192 pp, Quality PB, 978-1-58023-327-9 **$16.99**

Congregation Resources

Empowered Judaism: What Independent Minyanim Can Teach Us about Building Vibrant Jewish Communities
By Rabbi Elie Kaunfer; Foreword by Prof. Jonathan Sarna
Examines the independent minyan movement and what lessons these grassroots communities can provide. 6 x 9, 224 pp, Quality PB, 978-1-58023-412-2 **$18.99**

Spiritual Boredom: Rediscovering the Wonder of Judaism *By Dr. Erica Brown*
Breaks through the surface of spiritual boredom to find the reservoir of meaning within. 6 x 9, 208 pp, HC, 978-1-58023-405-4 **$21.99**

Building a Successful Volunteer Culture
Finding Meaning in Service in the Jewish Community
By Rabbi Charles Simon; Foreword by Shelley Lindauer; Preface by Dr. Ron Wolfson
Shows you how to develop and maintain the volunteers who are essential to the vitality of your organization and community. 6 x 9, 192 pp, Quality PB, 978-1-58023-408-5 **$16.99**

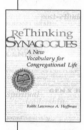

The Case for Jewish Peoplehood: Can We Be One?
By Dr. Erica Brown and Dr. Misha Galperin; Foreword by Rabbi Joseph Telushkin
6 x 9, 224 pp, HC, 978-1-58023-401-6 **$21.99**

Inspired Jewish Leadership: Practical Approaches to Building Strong Communities
By Dr. Erica Brown 6 x 9, 256 pp, HC, 978-1-58023-361-3 **$24.99**

Jewish Pastoral Care, 2nd Edition: A Practical Handbook from Traditional & Contemporary Sources *Edited by Rabbi Dayle A. Friedman, MSW, MAJCS, BCC*
6 x 9, 528 pp, Quality PB, 978-1-58023-427-6 **$30.00**; HC, 978-1-58023-221-0 **$40.00**

Rethinking Synagogues: A New Vocabulary for Congregational Life
By Rabbi Lawrence A. Hoffman 6 x 9, 240 pp, Quality PB, 978-1-58023-248-7 **$19.99**

The Spirituality of Welcoming: How to Transform Your Congregation into a Sacred Community *By Dr. Ron Wolfson* 6 x 9, 224 pp, Quality PB, 978-1-58023-244-9 **$19.99**

Children's Books

What You Will See Inside a Synagogue
By Rabbi Lawrence A. Hoffman, PhD, and Dr. Ron Wolfson; Full-color photos by Bill Aron
A colorful, fun-to-read introduction that explains the ways and whys of Jewish worship and religious life. 8½ x 10½, 32 pp, Full-color photos, Quality PB, 978-1-59473-256-0 **$8.99**
For ages 6 & up (A book from SkyLight Paths, Jewish Lights' sister imprint)

Because Nothing Looks Like God
By Lawrence Kushner and Karen Kushner Introduces children to the possibilities of spiritual life. 11 x 8½, 32 pp, Full-color illus., HC, 978-1-58023-092-6 **$17.99** *For ages 4 & up*

Board Book Companions to *Because Nothing Looks Like God*
5 x 5, 24 pp, Full-color illus., SkyLight Paths Board Books *For ages 0–4*

What Does God Look Like? 978-1-893361-23-2 **$7.99**

How Does God Make Things Happen? 978-1-893361-24-9 **$7.95**

Where Is God? 978-1-893361-17-1 **$7.99**

The Book of Miracles: A Young Person's Guide to Jewish Spiritual Awareness
Written and illus. by Lawrence Kushner
6 x 9, 96 pp, 2-color illus., HC, 978-1-879045-78-1 **$16.95** *For ages 9 & up*

In God's Hands
By Lawrence Kushner and Gary Schmidt 9 x 12, 32 pp, HC, 978-1-58023-224-1 **$16.99**

In Our Image: God's First Creatures *By Nancy Sohn Swartz*
9 x 12, 32 pp, Full-color illus., HC, 978-1-879045-99-6 **$16.95** *For ages 4 & up*

Also Available as a Board Book: **How Did the Animals Help God?**
5 x 5, 24 pp, Full-color illus., Board Book, 978-1-59473-044-3 **$7.99** *For ages 0–4*
(A book from SkyLight Paths, Jewish Lights' sister imprint)

The Kids' Fun Book of Jewish Time
By Emily Sper 9 x 7½, 24 pp, Full-color illus., HC, 978-1-58023-311-8 **$16.99**

What Makes Someone a Jew? *By Lauren Seidman*
Reflects the changing face of American Judaism.
10 x 8½, 32 pp, Full-color photos, Quality PB, 978-1-58023-321-7 **$8.99** *For ages 3–6*

Life Cycle

Marriage/Parenting/Family/Aging

The New Jewish Baby Album: Creating and Celebrating the Beginning of a Spiritual Life—A Jewish Lights Companion
By the Editors at Jewish Lights; Foreword by Anita Diamant; Preface by Rabbi Sandy Eisenberg Sasso
A spiritual keepsake that will be treasured for generations. More than just a memory book, *shows you how—and why it's important*—to create a Jewish home and a Jewish life. 8 x 10, 64 pp, Deluxe Padded HC, Full-color illus., 978-1-58023-138-1 **$19.95**

The Jewish Pregnancy Book: A Resource for the Soul, Body & Mind during Pregnancy, Birth & the First Three Months
By Sandy Falk, MD, and Rabbi Daniel Judson, with Steven A. Rapp
Includes medical information, prayers and rituals for each stage of pregnancy, from a liberal Jewish perspective. 7 x 10, 208 pp, b/w photos, Quality PB, 978-1-58023-178-7 **$16.95**

Celebrating Your New Jewish Daughter: Creating Jewish Ways to Welcome Baby Girls into the Covenant—New and Traditional Ceremonies *By Debra Nussbaum Cohen; Foreword by Rabbi Sandy Eisenberg Sasso* 6 x 9, 272 pp, Quality PB, 978-1-58023-090-2 **$18.95**

The New Jewish Baby Book, 2nd Edition: Names, Ceremonies & Customs—A Guide for Today's Families *By Anita Diamant* 6 x 9, 336 pp, Quality PB, 978-1-58023-251-7 **$19.99**

Parenting as a Spiritual Journey: Deepening Ordinary and Extraordinary Events into Sacred Occasions *By Rabbi Nancy Fuchs-Kreimer*
6 x 9, 224 pp, Quality PB, 978-1-58023-016-2 **$16.95**

Parenting Jewish Teens: A Guide for the Perplexed
By Joanne Doades
Explores the questions and issues that shape the world in which today's Jewish teenagers live and offers constructive advice to parents.
6 x 9, 176 pp, Quality PB, 978-1-58023-305-7 **$16.99**

Judaism for Two: A Spiritual Guide for Strengthening and Celebrating Your Loving Relationship *By Rabbi Nancy Fuchs-Kreimer, PhD, and Rabbi Nancy H. Wiener, DMin; Foreword by Rabbi Elliot N. Dorff*
Addresses the ways Jewish teachings can enhance and strengthen committed relationships. 6 x 9, 224 pp, Quality PB, 978-1-58023-254-8 **$16.99**

The Creative Jewish Wedding Book, 2nd Edition: A Hands-On Guide to New & Old Traditions, Ceremonies & Celebrations *By Gabrielle Kaplan-Mayer*
9 x 9, 288 pp, b/w photos, Quality PB, 978-1-58023-398-9 **$19.99**

Divorce Is a Mitzvah: A Practical Guide to Finding Wholeness and Holiness When Your Marriage Dies *By Rabbi Perry Netter; Afterword by Rabbi Laura Geller*
6 x 9, 224 pp, Quality PB, 978-1-58023-172-5 **$16.95**

Embracing the Covenant: Converts to Judaism Talk About Why & How
By Rabbi Allan Berkowitz and Patti Moskovitz 6 x 9, 192 pp, Quality PB, 978-1-879045-50-7 **$16.95**

The Guide to Jewish Interfaith Family Life: An InterfaithFamily.com Handbook *Edited by Ronnie Friedland and Edmund Case*
6 x 9, 384 pp, Quality PB, 978-1-58023-153-4 **$18.95**

A Heart of Wisdom: Making the Jewish Journey from Midlife through the Elder Years
Edited by Susan Berrin; Foreword by Harold Kushner
6 x 9, 384 pp, Quality PB, 978-1-58023-051-3 **$18.95**

Introducing My Faith and My Community
The Jewish Outreach Institute Guide for the Christian in a Jewish Interfaith Relationship
By Rabbi Kerry M. Olitzky 6 x 9, 176 pp, Quality PB, 978-1-58023-192-3 **$16.99**

Making a Successful Jewish Interfaith Marriage: The Jewish Outreach Institute Guide to Opportunities, Challenges and Resources *By Rabbi Kerry M. Olitzky with Joan Peterson Littman*
6 x 9, 176 pp, Quality PB, 978-1-58023-170-1 **$16.95**

So That Your Values Live On: Ethical Wills and How to Prepare Them
Edited by Jack Riemer and Nathaniel Stampfer
6 x 9, 272 pp, Quality PB, 978-1-879045-34-7 **$18.99**

Meditation

Jewish Meditation Practices for Everyday Life

Awakening Your Heart, Connecting with God
By Rabbi Jeff Roth
Offers a fresh take on meditation that draws on life experience and living life with greater clarity as opposed to the traditional method of rigorous study.
6 x 9, 224 pp, Quality PB Original, 978-1-58023-397-2 **$18.99**

The Handbook of Jewish Meditation Practices

A Guide for Enriching the Sabbath and Other Days of Your Life
By Rabbi David A. Cooper Easy-to-learn meditation techniques.
6 x 9, 208 pp, Quality PB, 978-1-58023-102-2 **$16.95**

Discovering Jewish Meditation: Instruction & Guidance for Learning an Ancient Spiritual Practice *By Nan Fink Gefen, PhD* 6 x 9, 208 pp, Quality PB, 978-1-58023-067-4 **$16.95**

Meditation from the Heart of Judaism: Today's Teachers Share Their Practices, Techniques, and Faith *Edited by Avram Davis*
6 x 9, 256 pp, Quality PB, 978-1-58023-049-0 **$16.95**

Ritual/Sacred Practices

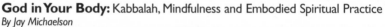

The Jewish Dream Book: The Key to Opening the Inner Meaning of Your Dreams *By Vanessa L. Ochs, PhD, with Elizabeth Ochs; Illus. by Kristina Swarner*
Instructions for how modern people can perform ancient Jewish dream practices and dream interpretations drawn from the Jewish wisdom tradition.
8 x 8, 128 pp, Full-color illus., Deluxe PB w/ flaps, 978-1-58023-132-9 **$16.95**

God in Your Body: Kabbalah, Mindfulness and Embodied Spiritual Practice
By Jay Michaelson
The first comprehensive treatment of the body in Jewish spiritual practice and an essential guide to the sacred.
6 x 9, 272 pp, Quality PB, 978-1-58023-304-0 **$18.99**

The Book of Jewish Sacred Practices: CLAL's Guide to Everyday & Holiday Rituals & Blessings *Edited by Rabbi Irwin Kula and Vanessa L. Ochs, PhD*
6 x 9, 368 pp, Quality PB, 978-1-58023-152-7 **$18.95**

Jewish Ritual: A Brief Introduction for Christians
By Rabbi Kerry M. Olitzky and Rabbi Daniel Judson
5½ x 8½, 144 pp, Quality PB, 978-1-58023-210-4 **$14.99**

The Rituals & Practices of a Jewish Life: A Handbook for Personal Spiritual Renewal *Edited by Rabbi Kerry M. Olitzky and Rabbi Daniel Judson*
6 x 9, 272 pp, illus., Quality PB, 978-1-58023-169-5 **$18.95**

The Sacred Art of Lovingkindness: Preparing to Practice
By Rabbi Rami Shapiro 5½ x 8½, 176 pp, Quality PB, 978-1-59473-151-8 **$16.99**
(A book from SkyLight Paths, Jewish Lights' sister imprint)

Science Fiction/Mystery & Detective Fiction

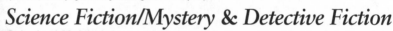

Criminal Kabbalah: An Intriguing Anthology of Jewish Mystery & Detective Fiction *Edited by Lawrence W. Raphael; Foreword by Laurie R. King*
All-new stories from twelve of today's masters of mystery and detective fiction—sure to delight mystery buffs of all faith traditions.
6 x 9, 256 pp, Quality PB, 978-1-58023-109-1 **$16.95**

Mystery Midrash: An Anthology of Jewish Mystery & Detective Fiction
Edited by Lawrence W. Raphael; Preface by Joel Siegel
6 x 9, 304 pp, Quality PB, 978-1-58023-055-1 **$16.95**

Wandering Stars: An Anthology of Jewish Fantasy & Science Fiction
Edited by Jack Dann; Introduction by Isaac Asimov
6 x 9, 272 pp, Quality PB, 978-1-58023-005-6 **$18.99**

More Wandering Stars: An Anthology of Outstanding Stories of Jewish Fantasy and Science Fiction *Edited by Jack Dann; Introduction by Isaac Asimov*
6 x 9, 192 pp, Quality PB, 978-1-58023-063-6 **$16.95**

Spirituality

Repentance: The Meaning and Practice of *Teshuvah*
By Dr. Louis E. Newman; Foreword by Rabbi Harold M. Schulweis; Preface by Rabbi Karyn D. Kedar
Examines both the practical and philosophical dimensions of *teshuvah*, Judaism's core religious-moral teaching on repentance, and its value for us—Jews and non-Jews alike—today. 6 x 9, 256 pp, HC, 978-1-58023-426-9 **$24.99**

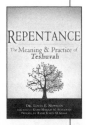

Tanya, the Masterpiece of Hasidic Wisdom
Selections Annotated & Explained
Translation & Annotation by Rabbi Rami Shapiro
Brings the genius of the *Tanya* to anyone seeking to deepen their understanding of the soul and how it relates to and manifests the Divine Source.
5½ x 8½, 192 pp (est), Quality PB, 978-1-59473-275-1 **$16.99**
(A book from SkyLight Paths, Jewish Lights' sister imprint)

A Book of Life: Embracing Judaism as a Spiritual Practice
By Rabbi Michael Strassfeld 6 x 9, 544 pp, Quality PB, 978-1-58023-247-0 **$19.99**

Meaning and Mitzvah: Daily Practices for Reclaiming Judaism through Prayer, God, Torah, Hebrew, Mitzvot and Peoplehood *By Rabbi Goldie Milgram*
7 x 9, 336 pp, Quality PB, 978-1-58023-256-2 **$19.99**

The Soul of the Story: Meetings with Remarkable People
By Rabbi David Zeller 6 x 9, 288 pp, HC, 978-1-58023-272-2 **$21.99**

Aleph-Bet Yoga: Embodying the Hebrew Letters for Physical and Spiritual Well-Being
By Steven A. Rapp; Foreword by Tamar Frankiel, PhD, and Judy Greenfeld; Preface by Hart Lazer
7 x 10, 128 pp, b/w photos, Quality PB, Layflat binding, 978-1-58023-162-6 **$16.95**

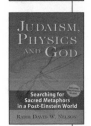

Does the Soul Survive? A Jewish Journey to Belief in Afterlife, Past Lives & Living with Purpose *By Rabbi Elie Kaplan Spitz; Foreword by Brian L. Weiss, MD*
6 x 9, 288 pp, Quality PB, 978-1-58023-165-7 **$16.99**

First Steps to a New Jewish Spirit: Reb Zalman's Guide to Recapturing the Intimacy & Ecstasy in Your Relationship with God *By Rabbi Zalman M. Schachter-Shalomi with Donald Gropman* 6 x 9, 144 pp, Quality PB, 978-1-58023-182-4 **$16.95**

Foundations of Sephardic Spirituality: The Inner Life of Jews of the Ottoman Empire
By Rabbi Marc D. Angel, PhD 6 x 9, 224 pp, Quality PB, 978-1-58023-341-5 **$18.99**

God in Our Relationships: Spirituality between People from the Teachings of Martin Buber *By Rabbi Dennis S. Ross* 5½ x 8½, 160 pp, Quality PB, 978-1-58023-147-3 **$16.95**

Judaism, Physics and God: Searching for Sacred Metaphors in a Post-Einstein World
By Rabbi David W. Nelson 6 x 9, 352 pp, Quality PB, inc. reader's discussion guide, 978-1-58023-306-4 **$18.99**; HC, 352 pp, 978-1-58023-252-4 **$24.99**

The Jewish Lights Spirituality Handbook: A Guide to Understanding, Exploring & Living a Spiritual Life *Edited by Stuart M. Matlins*
What exactly is "Jewish" about spirituality? How do I make it a part of my life? Fifty of today's foremost spiritual leaders share their ideas and experience with us.
6 x 9, 456 pp, Quality PB, 978-1-58023-093-3 **$19.99**

Bringing the Psalms to Life: How to Understand and Use the Book of Psalms
By Rabbi Daniel F. Polish, PhD 6 x 9, 208 pp, Quality PB, 978-1-58023-157-2 **$16.95**

God & the Big Bang: Discovering Harmony between Science & Spirituality
By Dr. Daniel C. Matt 6 x 9, 216 pp, Quality PB, 978-1-879045-89-7 **$16.99**

Minding the Temple of the Soul: Balancing Body, Mind, and Spirit through Traditional Jewish Prayer, Movement, and Meditation *By Tamar Frankiel, PhD, and Judy Greenfeld*
7 x 10, 184 pp, illus., Quality PB, 978-1-879045-64-4 **$16.95**

One God Clapping: The Spiritual Path of a Zen Rabbi *By Alan Lew with Sherril Jaffe*
5½ x 8½, 336 pp, Quality PB, 978-1-58023-115-2 **$16.95**

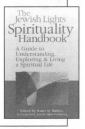

There Is No Messiah ... and You're It: The Stunning Transformation of Judaism's Most Provocative Idea *By Rabbi Robert N. Levine, DD*
6 x 9, 192 pp, Quality PB, 978-1-58023-255-5 **$16.99**

These Are the Words: A Vocabulary of Jewish Spiritual Life
By Rabbi Arthur Green, PhD 6 x 9, 304 pp, Quality PB, 978-1-58023-107-7 **$18.95**

Theology/Philosophy

Jewish Theology in Our Time: A New Generation Explores the Foundations and Future of Jewish Belief *Edited by Rabbi Elliot J. Cosgrove, PhD*
A powerful and challenging examination of what Jews can believe—by a new generation's most dynamic and innovative thinkers.
6 x 9, 350 pp (est), HC, 978-1-58023-413-9 **$24.99**

Maimonides, Spinoza and Us: Toward an Intellectually Vibrant Judaism *By Rabbi Marc D. Angel, PhD* A challenging look at two great Jewish philosophers, and what their thinking means to our understanding of God, truth, revelation and reason. 6 x 9, 224 pp, HC, 978-1-58023-411-5 **$24.99**

A Touch of the Sacred: A Theologian's Informal Guide to Jewish Belief *By Dr. Eugene B. Borowitz and Frances W. Schwartz*
Explores the musings from the leading theologian of liberal Judaism.
6 x 9, 256 pp, Quality PB, 978-1-58023-416-0 **$16.99**; HC, 978-1-58023-337-8 **$21.99**

Jews and Judaism in the 21st Century: Human Responsibility, the Presence of God, and the Future of the Covenant *Edited by Rabbi Edward Feinstein; Foreword by Paula E. Hyman* Five celebrated leaders in Judaism examine contemporary Jewish life. 6 x 9, 192 pp, Quality PB, 978-1-58023-374-3 **$19.99**; HC, 978-1-58023-315-6 **$24.99**

The Death of Death: Resurrection and Immortality in Jewish Thought
By Rabbi Neil Gillman, PhD 6 x 9, 336 pp, Quality PB, 978-1-58023-081-0 **$18.95**

Ethics of the Sages: Pirke Avot—Annotated & Explained
Translation & Annotation by Rabbi Rami Shapiro
5½ x 8½, 192 pp, Quality PB, 978-1-59473-207-2 **$16.99** (A book from SkyLight Paths, Jewish Lights' sister imprint)

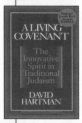

Hasidic Tales: Annotated & Explained *Translation & Annotation by Rabbi Rami Shapiro*
5½ x 8½, 240 pp, Quality PB, 978-1-893361-86-7 **$16.95** (A book from SkyLight Paths, Jewish Lights' sister imprint)

A Heart of Many Rooms: Celebrating the Many Voices within Judaism
By Dr. David Hartman 6 x 9, 352 pp, Quality PB, 978-1-58023-156-5 **$19.95**

The Hebrew Prophets: Selections Annotated & Explained
Translation & Annotation by Rabbi Rami Shapiro; Foreword by Rabbi Zalman M. Schachter-Shalomi
5½ x 8½, 224 pp, Quality PB, 978-1-59473-037-5 **$16.99** (A book from SkyLight Paths, Jewish Lights' sister imprint)

A Jewish Understanding of the New Testament
By Rabbi Samuel Sandmel; Preface by Rabbi David Sandmel
5½ x 8½, 368 pp, Quality PB, 978-1-59473-048-1 **$19.99** (A book from SkyLight Paths, Jewish Lights' sister imprint)

Keeping Faith with the Psalms: Deepen Your Relationship with God Using the Book of Psalms *By Rabbi Daniel F. Polish, PhD* 6 x 9, 320 pp, Quality PB, 978-1-58023-300-2 **$18.99**

A Living Covenant: The Innovative Spirit in Traditional Judaism
By Dr. David Hartman 6 x 9, 368 pp, Quality PB, 978-1-58023-011-7 **$20.00**

Love and Terror in the God Encounter: The Theological Legacy of Rabbi Joseph B. Soloveitchik *By Dr. David Hartman* 6 x 9, 240 pp, Quality PB, 978-1-58023-176-3 **$19.95**

The Personhood of God: Biblical Theology, Human Faith and the Divine Image
By Dr. Yochanan Muffs; Foreword by Dr. David Hartman
6 x 9, 240 pp, Quality PB, 978-1-58023-338-5 **$18.99**; HC, 978-1-58023-265-4 **$24.99**

Traces of God: Seeing God in Torah, History and Everyday Life *By Rabbi Neil Gillman, PhD*
6 x 9, 240 pp, Quality PB, 978-1-58023-369-9 **$16.99**; HC, 978-1-58023-249-4 **$21.99**

We Jews and Jesus: Exploring Theological Differences for Mutual Understanding
By Rabbi Samuel Sandmel; Preface by Rabbi David Sandmel
6 x 9, 192 pp, Quality PB, 978-1-59473-208-9 **$16.99** (A book from SkyLight Paths, Jewish Lights' sister imprint)

Your Word Is Fire: The Hasidic Masters on Contemplative Prayer
Edited and translated by Rabbi Arthur Green, PhD, and Barry W. Holtz
6 x 9, 160 pp, Quality PB, 978-1-879045-25-5 **$15.95**

I Am Jewish
Personal Reflections Inspired by the Last Words of Daniel Pearl
Almost 150 Jews—both famous and not—from all walks of life, from all around the world, write about many aspects of their Judaism.
Edited by Judea and Ruth Pearl 6 x 9, 304 pp, Deluxe PB w/ flaps, 978-1-58023-259-3 **$18.99**
Download a free copy of the *I Am Jewish Teacher's Guide* at www.jewishlights.com.

Social Justice

There Shall Be No Needy
Pursuing Social Justice through Jewish Law and Tradition
By Rabbi Jill Jacobs; Foreword by Rabbi Elliot N. Dorff, PhD; Preface by Simon Greer
Confronts the most pressing issues of twenty-first-century America from a deeply
Jewish perspective.
6 x 9, 288 pp, Quality PB, 978-1-58023-425-2 **$16.99**; HC, 978-1-58023-394-1 **$21.99**

Conscience: The Duty to Obey and the Duty to Disobey
By Rabbi Harold M. Schulweis
This clarion call to rethink our moral and political behavior examines the idea of
conscience and the role conscience plays in our relationships to governments, law,
ethics, religion, human nature, God—and to each other.
6 x 9, 160 pp, Quality PB, 978-1-58023-419-1 **$16.99**; HC, 978-1-58023-375-0 **$19.99**

Judaism and Justice: The Jewish Passion to Repair the World
By Rabbi Sidney Schwarz; Foreword by Ruth Messinger
Explores the relationship between Judaism, social justice and the Jewish identity
of American Jews.
6 x 9, 352 pp, Quality PB, 978-1-58023-353-8 **$19.99**; HC, 978-1-58023-312-5 **$24.99**

Spiritual Activism: A Jewish Guide to Leadership and Repairing the World
By Rabbi Avraham Weiss; Foreword by Alan M. Dershowitz
6 x 9, 224 pp, Quality PB, 978-1-58023-418-4 **$16.99**; HC, 978-1-58023-355-2 **$24.99**

Righteous Indignation: A Jewish Call for Justice
Edited by Rabbi Or N. Rose, Jo Ellen Green Kaiser and Margie Klein; Foreword by Rabbi David Ellenson
Leading progressive Jewish activists explore meaningful intellectual and spiritual
foundations for their social justice work.
6 x 9, 384 pp, Quality PB, 978-1-58023-414-6 **$19.99**; HC, 978-1-58023-336-1 **$24.99**

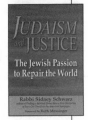

Spirituality/Women's Interest

New Jewish Feminism: Probing the Past, Forging the Future
Edited by Rabbi Elyse Goldstein; Foreword by Anita Diamant
Looks at the growth and accomplishments of Jewish feminism and what they
mean for Jewish women today and tomorrow.
6 x 9, 480 pp, HC, 978-1-58023-359-0 **$24.99**

The Quotable Jewish Woman: Wisdom, Inspiration & Humor from the Mind & Heart
Edited by Elaine Bernstein Partnow
6 x 9, 496 pp, Quality PB, 978-1-58023-236-4 **$19.99**

The Divine Feminine in Biblical Wisdom Literature
Selections Annotated & Explained
Translated and Annotated by Rabbi Rami Shapiro
5½ x 8½, 240 pp, Quality PB, 978-1-59473-109-9 **$16.99**
(A book from SkyLight Paths, Jewish Lights' sister imprint)

The Women's Haftarah Commentary: New Insights from Women
Rabbis on the 54 Weekly Haftarah Portions, the 5 Megillot & Special Shabbatot
Edited by Rabbi Elyse Goldstein
Illuminates the historical significance of female portrayals in the Haftarah and the
Five Megillot.
6 x 9, 560 pp, Quality PB, 978-1-58023-371-2 **$19.99**; HC, 978-1-58023-133-6 **$39.99**

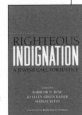

The Women's Torah Commentary: New Insights from Women
Rabbis on the 54 Weekly Torah Portions
Edited by Rabbi Elyse Goldstein
Over fifty women rabbis offer inspiring insights on the Torah, in a week-by-week format.
6 x 9, 496 pp, Quality PB, 978-1-58023-370-5 **$19.99**; HC, 978-1-58023-076-6 **$34.95**

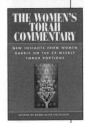

Inspiration

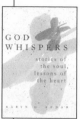

The Seven Questions You're Asked in Heaven: Reviewing and Renewing Your Life on Earth *By Dr. Ron Wolfson*
An intriguing and entertaining resource for living a life that matters.
6 x 9, 176 pp, Quality PB, 978-1-58023-407-8 **$16.99**

Happiness and the Human Spirit: The Spirituality of Becoming the Best You Can Be *By Abraham J. Twerski, MD*
Shows you that true happiness is attainable once you stop looking outside yourself for the source. 6 x 9, 176 pp, Quality PB, 978-1-58023-404-7 **$16.99**; HC, 978-1-58023-343-9 **$19.99**

Life's Daily Blessings: Inspiring Reflections on Gratitude and Joy for Every Day, Based on Jewish Wisdom *By Rabbi Kerry M. Olitzky* 4½ x 6½, 368 pp, Quality PB, 978-1-58023-396-5 **$16.99**

The Bridge to Forgiveness: Stories and Prayers for Finding God and Restoring Wholeness *By Rabbi Karyn D. Kedar*
Examines how forgiveness can be the bridge that connects us to wholeness and peace.
6 x 9, 176 pp, HC, 978-1-58023-324-8 **$19.99**

A Formula for Proper Living: Practical Lessons from Life and Torah
By Abraham J. Twerski, MD
Gives you practical lessons for life that you can put to day-to-day use in dealing with yourself and others. 6 x 9, 144 pp, HC, 978-1-58023-402-3 **$19.99**

God's To-Do List: 103 Ways to Be an Angel and Do God's Work on Earth
By Dr. Ron Wolfson 6 x 9, 144 pp, Quality PB, 978-1-58023-301-9 **$16.99**

The Empty Chair: Finding Hope and Joy—Timeless Wisdom from a Hasidic Master, Rebbe Nachman of Breslov *Adapted by Moshe Mykoff and the Breslov Research Institute*
4 x 6, 128 pp, Deluxe PB w/ flaps, 978-1-879045-67-5 **$9.99**

The Gentle Weapon: Prayers for Everyday and Not-So-Everyday Moments—Timeless Wisdom from the Teachings of the Hasidic Master, Rebbe Nachman of Breslov
Adapted by Moshe Mykoff and S. C. Mizrahi, together with the Breslov Research Institute
4 x 6, 144 pp, Deluxe PB w/ flaps, 978-1-58023-022-3 **$9.99**

God Whispers: Stories of the Soul, Lessons of the Heart *By Karyn D. Kedar*
6 x 9, 176 pp, Quality PB, 978-1-58023-088-9 **$15.95**

Restful Reflections: Nighttime Inspiration to Calm the Soul, Based on Jewish Wisdom
By Rabbi Kerry M. Olitzky and Rabbi Lori Forman 4½ x 6½, 448 pp, Quality PB, 978-1-58023-091-9 **$15.95**

Sacred Intentions: Daily Inspiration to Strengthen the Spirit, Based on Jewish Wisdom
By Rabbi Kerry M. Olitzky and Rabbi Lori Forman 4½ x 6½, 448 pp, Quality PB, 978-1-58023-061-2 **$15.95**

Kabbalah/Mysticism

Seek My Face: A Jewish Mystical Theology *By Arthur Green*
6 x 9, 304 pp, Quality PB, 978-1-58023-130-5 **$19.95**

Zohar: Annotated & Explained *Translation & Annotation by Daniel C. Matt;*
Foreword by Andrew Harvey 5½ x 8½, 176 pp, Quality PB, 978-1-893361-51-5 **$15.99**
(A book from SkyLight Paths, Jewish Lights' sister imprint)

Ehyeh: A Kabbalah for Tomorrow
By Arthur Green 6 x 9, 224 pp, Quality PB, 978-1-58023-213-5 **$16.99**

The Flame of the Heart: Prayers of a Chasidic Mystic
By Reb Noson of Breslov; Translated and adapted by David Sears, with the Breslov Research Institute
5 x 7¼, 160 pp, Quality PB, 978-1-58023-246-3 **$15.99**

The Gift of Kabbalah: Discovering the Secrets of Heaven, Renewing Your Life on Earth
By Tamar Frankiel, PhD 6 x 9, 256 pp, Quality PB, 978-1-58023-141-1 **$16.95**

Kabbalah: A Brief Introduction for Christians
By Tamar Frankiel, PhD 5½ x 8½, 208 pp, Quality PB, 978-1-58023-303-3 **$16.99**

The Lost Princess & Other Kabbalistic Tales of Rebbe Nachman of Breslov
The Seven Beggars & Other Kabbalistic Tales of Rebbe Nachman of Breslov
Translated by Rabbi Aryeh Kaplan; Preface by Rabbi Chaim Kramer
Lost Princess: 6 x 9, 400 pp, Quality PB, 978-1-58023-217-3 **$18.99**
Seven Beggars: 6 x 9, 192 pp, Quality PB, 978-1-58023-250-0 **$16.99**

Pastoral Care Resources
LifeLights/™אורות החיים

LifeLights/™אורות החיים are inspirational, informational booklets about challenges to our emotional and spiritual lives and how to deal with them. Offering help for wholeness and healing, each *LifeLight* is written from a uniquely Jewish spiritual perspective by a wise and caring soul—someone who knows the inner territory of grief, doubt, confusion and longing.

In addition to providing wise words to light a difficult path, each *LifeLight* booklet provides suggestions for additional resources for reading. Many list organizations, Jewish and secular, that can provide help, along with information on how to contact them.

Categories/Sample Topics:

Health & Healing
Caring for Yourself/When Someone Is Ill
Facing Cancer as a Family
Recognizing a Loved One's Addiction, and Providing Help

Loss / Grief / Death & Dying
Coping with the Death of a Spouse
From Death through Shiva: A Guide to Jewish Grieving Practices
Taking the Time You Need to Mourn Your Loss
Talking to Children about Death

Judaism / Living a Jewish Life
Bar and Bat Mitzvah's Meaning: Preparing Spiritually with Your Child
Yearning for God

Family Issues
Grandparenting Interfaith Grandchildren
Talking to Your Children about God

Spiritual Care / Personal Growth
Easing the Burden of Stress
Finding a Way to Forgive
Praying in Hard Times

Now available in hundreds of congregations, health-care facilities, funeral homes, colleges and military installations, these helpful, comforting resources can be uniquely presented in *LifeLights* display racks, available from Jewish Lights. **Each *LifeLight* topic is sold in packs of twelve for $9.95.** General discounts are available for quantity purchases.

Visit us online at **www.jewishlights.com** for a complete list of titles, authors, prices and ordering information, or call us at (802) 457-4000 or toll free at (800) 962-4544.

About Jewish Lights

People of all faiths and backgrounds yearn for books that attract, engage, educate, and spiritually inspire.

Our principal goal is to stimulate thought and help all people learn about who the Jewish People are, where they come from, and what the future can be made to hold. While people of our diverse Jewish heritage are the primary audience, our books speak to people in the Christian world as well and will broaden their understanding of Judaism and the roots of their own faith.

We bring to you authors who are at the forefront of spiritual thought and experience. While each has something different to say, they all say it in a voice that you can hear.

Our books are designed to welcome you and then to engage, stimulate, and inspire. We judge our success not only by whether or not our books are beautiful and commercially successful, but by whether or not they make a difference in your life.

For your information and convenience, at the back of this book we have provided a list of other Jewish Lights books you might find interesting and useful. They cover all the categories of your life:

Bar/Bat Mitzvah	Life Cycle
Bible Study / Midrash	Meditation
Children's Books	Men's Interest
Congregation Resources	Parenting
Current Events / History	Prayer / Ritual / Sacred Practice
Ecology / Environment	Social Justice
Fiction: Mystery, Science Fiction	Spirituality
Grief / Healing	Theology / Philosophy
Holidays / Holy Days	Travel
Inspiration	12-Step
Kabbalah / Mysticism / Enneagram	Women's Interest

Stuart M. Matlins, Publisher